W9-BXD-282

DISCARD

NATIVE TRIBES OF
CALIFORNIA AND THE SOUTHWEST

Michael Johnson
& Bill Yenne

WORLD ALMANAC® LIBRARY

Please visit our web site at: www.worldalmanaclibrary.com
For a free color catalog describing World Almanac® Library's list
of high-quality books and multimedia programs, call 1-800-848-2928 (USA)
or 1-800-387-3178 (Canada). World Almanac® Library's fax: (414) 332-3567.

Library of Congress Cataloging-in-Publication Data

Johnson, Michael, 1937 Apr. 22-
    Native tribes of California and the Southwest / by Michael Johnson and Bill Yenne.
      p. cm. — (Native tribes of North America)
    Summary: An introduction to the history, culture, and people of the many Indian tribes that inhabited the region from northern California through the states
of New Mexico and Arizona and adjacent parts of Mexico and Texas.
    Includes bibliographical references and index.
    ISBN 0-8368-5609-0 (lib. bdg.)
    1. Indians of North America—Southwest, New—History—Juvenile literature. 2. Indians of North America—Southwest, New—Social life and customs—
Juvenile literature. 3. Indians of North America—California—History—Juvenile literature. 4. Indians of North America—California—Social life and
customs—Juvenile literature. [1. Indians of North America—Southwest, New. 2. Indians of North America—California.] I. Yenne, Bill, 1949– . II. Title.
    E78.S7J55 2004
    979.004'97—dc22
                                       2003060453

This North American edition first published in 2004 by
World Almanac® Library
330 West Olive Street, Suite 100
Milwaukee, WI 53212 USA

For Compendium Publishing
Contributors: Michael Johnson and Bill Yenne
Editor: Michael Burke
Picture research: Michael Johnson, Bill Yenne, and Simon Forty
Design: Tony Stocks/Compendium Design
Maps: Mark Franklin

World Almanac® Library editor: Barbara Kiely Miller
World Almanac® Library graphic designer: Steve Schraenkler

Picture credits
All artwork (other than maps) reproduced by kind permission of Richard Hook. All photographs are by Michael Johnson or supplied from his
collection unless credited otherwise below. Particular thanks are due to the staff of Royal Albert Memorial Museum and Art Gallery, Exeter, Devon,
U.K., for assistance and access to its exhibits, archives, and excellent collections, and to Bill Yenne for material of his own and from his collection.
Much of the material in this book appeared as part of *The Encyclopedia of Native Tribes of North America* by M. J. Johnson and
R. Hook, published by Compendium Publishing Ltd. in 2001.

Cambridge University Museum of Archaeology and Anthropology, U.K.: p. 52 (below); Royal Albert Memorial Museum and Art Gallery: pp. 1, 54;
Werner Forman Archive: pp. 4, 6, 57 (Phoebe Apperson Hearst Museum of Anthropology); Courtesy Ray Whiteway-Roberts: pp. 34, 36; Bill Yenne:
pp. 9, 25, 29, 33, 35 (below), 37, 42, 43 (above), 45 (below), 49, 52 (above).

Printed in the United States of America

1 2 3 4 5 6 7 8 9 08 07 06 05 04

Cover: An Apache woman wearing a two-piece buckskin dress and skirt, standing in front of a brush wickiup, c. 1880.

Previous Page: Californian headdress.

Contents

Introduction

Above: **The Rio Grande River.**

For thousands of years, the people known today as Native Americans or American Indians have inhabited the whole of the Americas, from Alaska to the southernmost tip of South America. Most scholars and anthropologists think that the ancestors of Native peoples came to the Americas from Asia over a land mass connecting Siberia and Alaska. These first Americans may have arrived as long as 30,000 years ago, although most historians estimate that this migration took place 15,000 years ago.

According to this theory, Paleo-Indians (*paleo*, from a Greek word meaning "ancient") migrated over many years down through an ice-free corridor in North America, spreading out from west to east and southward into Central and South America. In time, they inhabited the entire Western Hemisphere from north to south. Their descendants became the many diverse Native peoples encountered by European explorers and settlers.

"INDIANS" VS. "NATIVE AMERICANS"

Christopher Columbus is said to have "discovered" the Americas in 1492. But did he? Columbus was not the first European to visit what became known as the New World; Viking mariners had sailed to Greenland and Newfoundland almost five hundred years before and even founded short-lived colonies. Using the word "discovered" also ignores the fact that North America was already inhabited by Native civilizations whose ancestors had "discovered" the Americas for themselves.

When Columbus landed on an island he called San Salvador (Spanish for "Holy Savior"), he thought he had reached China or Japan. He had sailed west intending to get to the East—to Asia, or the fabled "Indies," as it was often called by Europeans of the time. Although he landed in the Bahamas, Columbus never really gave up on the idea that he had made it to the Indies. Thus when Native people first encountered Columbus and his men in the islands off Florida, the lost explorer called them "Indians." The original names that each tribal group had already given to themselves usually translate into English as "the people" or "human beings." Today, some Native people of North

America prefer to be called "American Indians," while others prefer "Native Americans." In this book, Native peoples will be referred to by their tribal names or, in more general cases, as "Indians."

Today's Indians are descended from cultures of great historical depth, diversity, and complexity. Their ancient ancestors, the Paleo-Indians, developed beliefs and behavior patterns that enabled them to survive in unpredictable and often harsh environments. These early hunter-gatherers had a close relationship with the land and a sense of absolute and eternal belonging to it. To them, everything in their world—trees, mountains, rivers, sky, animals, rock formations—had "spirit power," which they respected and placated through prayers and rituals in order to ensure their survival. These beliefs evolved over time into a fascinating and diverse series of creation stories, trickster tales, songs, prayers, and rituals passed down to and practiced by tribes throughout North America. Although many Indians today practice Christianity and other religions as well, many of their traditional songs, stories, dances, and other practices survive, on reservations and in areas where substantial tribal groups still live.

A CONTINENT OF CULTURES

Long before the Europeans arrived, important Indian cultures had already developed and disappeared. The ancient Adena and Hopewell people, for example, built a number of extraordinary burial mounds, and later even large towns, some of whose remains can still be seen at sites in the Midwest and South. These cultures were themselves gradually influenced by Mesoamerican (pre-Columbian Mexican and Central American) farming cultures based on growing maize (Indian corn), beans, and squash. They became the Mississippian culture from 700 A.D. The great spread of language groups across the North American continent also points to a rich Indian history of continual movement, invasion, migration, and conquest that took place long before European contact.

By the time the first European explorers and colonists set foot in North America, Indians had settled across the vast continent into different tribal groups and cultures that were active, energetic, and continually changing. American Indians were skilled in exploiting their particular

U.S. INDIAN POPULATION

There is no record of the number of Indians living north of the Rio Grande before Europeans came. A conservative estimate of Indian population made by ethnographer James Mooney is about 1,250,000 for the late sixteenth century, before the founding of Jamestown and Plymouth. Others have suggested figures as high as six million, although two to three million might be more realistic. The highest concentrations of people were in the coastal regions: the Atlantic slope in the East, along the Gulf of Mexico in the South, and in California in the West. Indians living in these areas also suffered the most from European diseases and from conflict with European colonists. Population figures for the twentieth century vary considerably, due mainly to U.S. government criteria used to determine who is or is not an Indian. Also, the U.S. Bureau of Indian Affairs (BIA), the official bureaucracy in charge of the remaining Indian lands and federal services to Indians, has few relations with Indians in certain states. Thus the BIA's population figures tend to be lower than those reported by the U.S. Census. In 1950, the BIA reported 396,000 enrolled Indians, of whom 245,000 were resident on reservations. The U.S. Census reported 827,108 Indians in 1970 and 1,418,195 in 1980. Census 2000 recorded 2,409,578 respondents who reported as American Indian or Alaskan Native only and identified a single tribe of origin.

Above: **The spectacular Mesa Verde, a famous Anasazi site.**

environments in a multitude of ways developed over time. They were also good at incorporating new methods and technologies from other peoples. When Europeans came, many Indians adapted the newcomers' technology to their own way of life, incorporating, for example, the horse, the rifle, money, beads, fabric, steel implements, and European-style agriculture into their own traditional cultures. In many cases, however, the benefits of European influence were eventually overshadowed by the displacement or outright destruction of traditional Native life.

WHAT THIS BOOK COVERS

The purpose of this book is to give some relevant facts about each of the main tribes native to most of California, the southwestern United States, and parts of Mexico. Included here are brief historical sketches of the tribes, descriptions of tribal language relationships and groups, and accounts of traditional cultures, tribal locations, and populations in early and recent times. Interaction with invading Europeans is shown in discussions of trade, wars, treaties, and the eventual Indian removal to lands whose boundaries served more to keep Indians in than to keep white settlers out. Today's political boundaries were not recognized by Indians on their original lands; their "borders" were defined by shifting areas of hunting, gathering, and farming that Native groups used and fought over. For ease of reference, however, tribal locations given here refer to modern U.S. and Canadian place names.

CALIFORNIA

Culturally speaking, the pre-European-contact Native civilizations that we refer to as "Californian" include lands that lie west of the Sierra Nevada and west of the Mojave Desert. East of the Sierra Nevada lies the Great Basin. From the Mojave east to west Texas is the Southwest. The remaining regions of what is now California are associated with other cultural areas. The Eastern Mono and Paiute living on the eastern side of the Sierra Nevada are part of the Basin. The tribes in the northwestern section are sometimes grouped with the Northwest Coast culture because of their wealth accumulation traits, prestige displays, and World Renewal rituals, such as the White Deerskin ceremonies.

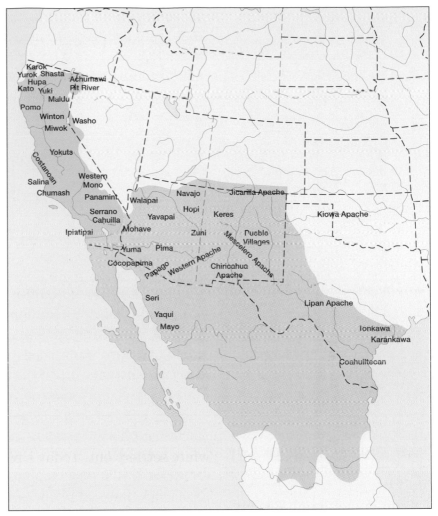

Wooden house types, dugout canoes, salmon fishing techniques, and twined basketry also reflect the northern culture.

Tribes in the southeastern portion of California had cultural affinities with the Southwest, such as coiled basketry and communal dwellings. Toloache, or the jimsonweed religion, was found in most of the area, with visions resulting from a toloache drink. Boys and girls had initiation ceremonies with religious and moral instructions from tribal chiefs.

The cultural characteristics typical of the Californian area were those found among the tribes who lived along the two main valley systems, those of the Sacramento and San Joaquin Rivers, including the eastern slopes of the Sierra Nevada north to Mount Shasta, and west to beyond Clear Lake and the Coast Range. In terms of linguistic diversity the area was one of the most complex in North America. The principal families included the Maidu, Wintun, Miwok, Costanoan, and Yokuts, who spoke related languages in the Penutian family; and the Karok, Shasta, Achumawi, Yana, Pomo, and others, whose language was Hokan. Living along the central and southern coast—in and near what are now the counties of Santa Barbara and San Luis Obispo—and in the Channel Islands, were the Hokan-speaking Chumash

Above: **The area covered in this book is largely, but not entirely, the present state of California and the states of New Mexico and Arizona plus adjacent parts of Mexico and Texas.**

PUEBLO

An Indian village in New Mexico or Arizona. Most northern Rio Grande community dwellings are made of sun-dried mud, or adobe, and straw bricks, forming honeycombs of rooms, sometimes terraced; the walls, thickly plastered with mud inside and out, are often whitewashed. Acoma, however, is of rubble and clay, while Zuñi Pueblo is of both stone and adobe bricks. Hopi towns have walls of dressed stone laid in adobe. These are almost the only pre-contact towns, but many others are near ancient sites. Most have plazas for public dances and subterranean kivas for secret rituals. Traditionally each clan of a tribe lives in one section of the building. Nowadays most rooms have doors and windows, but historically access was only by ladders through upper floors. Taos (above), perhaps the most impressive of these towns, is in parts six stories high.

people. They are noted for constructing large, oceangoing boats, which were used for fishing.

Food was mainly gathered and included vegetables, acorns, buckeye nuts, seeds, and a variety of grasses. The early Californians dug roots and bulbs from the ground and collected kelp and seaweed from the ocean, often drying or boiling these for soups. They hunted rabbits, quail, and gophers, collected grasshoppers and caterpillars, and fished for salmon. Houses were built of either coarse grass or bunches of tule reeds in dome shapes or, among the coastal people, of redwood plank slabs in conical shapes. Due to the generally mild climate, clothing was sparse—except for elaborate ceremonial dress using abalone shells, feathers, and skirts of vegetable fiber or deerskin. Some members also decorated their bodies with tattoos. Many tribes were excellent basket makers, and the Pomos made reed canoes at Clear Lake.

In central California, religion centered on the worship of ancestral ghosts through the Kuksu cult, a society of spirit or ancestral impersonation involving colorful attire and the initiation of youths by ghosts. Old men with special knowledge often acted as directors, including instruction on morals, hero gods, and healing. A variant religion among the Patwin people was known as the Hesi. Ceremonies usually took place in large circular semi-underground wooden buildings. These religions were influenced by other Indian spiritual movements in the second half of the 1800s, such as the Ghost Dance of 1870, the Earth Lodge Cult, and the Bole-Maru "Dream Dance."

The decrease in the Native population has been the greatest in California. Before European arrival, the population was over 300,000, but by 1910 there were no more than 25,000, and many of these were of mixed ancestry. The coastal and central valley tribes suffered the most—the former as a result of Spanish colonization, the latter due to the influx of gold-seekers after 1849, when villages were broken up and Indian peoples driven from their land (and often killed) in quasi-military clearance operations. Only where substantial reservations were created did the Native people survive in sizable groups. Many were left without land, engulfed by white culture and communities into which many small groups merged.

Government intervention in the late nineteenth and early twentieth centuries, notably the passage of the Rancheria Act of 1884, led to the foundation of small reservations around the state called *rancherias*. These gave a few hundred people a land base, but more lived scattered among the white population. Today, California has the largest Indian population of any state. People in California identifying themselves with a specific American Indian tribe numbered 201,311 in 1980 and 322,001 in 2000. The majority of them, however, were people whose ethnicity was associated with tribes that were not part of the traditional, pre-twentieth-century California culture.

THE SOUTHWEST

Culturally speaking, the Southwest comprises primarily the modern states of Arizona and New Mexico. This area also extends, however, to include people living in the desert regions of what is now southeastern California, southern Utah, southern Colorado, as well as parts of west Texas and northern Mexico. The historic Southwest culture derives basically from two sources: one an ancient agricultural tradition, the other a much later northern hunting tradition, introduced from about A.D. 1400 by the Athabascan-speaking Navajo and Apache, relative newcomers to the area. Three major prehistoric cultures contributed to the older cultural traditions of the region: the Mogollon and Hohokam, which preceded the Pima and Papago, and the Anasazi, which preceded the Pueblo.

The Mogollon culture, c. 500 B.C.–A.D. 1400, adopted agriculture and pottery from what is now Mexico.

CENSUS 2000 FIGURES

Wherever possible, U.S. Census 2000 figures are supplied with each entry showing how many people identified themselves as American Indian or Alaskan Native alone and members of one tribe. Other information regarding American Indians or Alaskan Natives, in combination with one or more races and reporting more than one tribe of origin, can be studied by examining the census returns. Reporting variables mean that some of the totals published here may not be the precise sum of the individual elements.

Left: **Taos Pueblo, New Mexico. It is probably the most spectacular Rio Grande Pueblo Indian village still occupied.**

Below: **Hopis have lived in the same area of northeastern Arizona for over 1,600 years.**

Below: **Santa Clara Pueblo, Rainbow Dance, c. 1960. Santa Clara is the third-largest of the six northern Tewa-speaking Pueblo towns located on the west bank of the Rio Grande between Taos and Santa Fe, New Mexico.**

Members of this culture were mainly pit-house farmers and the originators of later developments in the Southwest. The Mogollon culture began in Cochise County, Arizona, and spread to neighboring areas.

Hohokam culture, c. 300 B.C.–A.D. 1450, developed farther west, along the Gila River around the site of modern Phoenix. The Hohokam people developed irrigation canal systems, fine pottery, and stonework. Both the Mogollon and Hohokam cultures declined during the early fifteenth century, and the modern Pima and Papago tribes are most probably their descendants.

The Anasazi ("ancient ones") is a collective term to cover a people who lived at sites within eastern Arizona, western New Mexico, and adjacent Colorado from about 250 B.C. to about A.D. 1700. The earliest phases are termed "Basketmaker," 250 B.C.–A.D. 700, and "Modified Basketmaker," A.D. 400–700. These were followed by three Pueblo periods: first the "Development Period;" then the "Great Pueblo Period," characterized by large towns with fine masonry apartments, which were abandoned in about A.D. 1276 when the people moved south to the Hopi and Zuñi pueblos and the Rio Grande; and finally, the "Regressive Pueblo Period," A.D. 1300–1700. The Anasazi may have left their cliffside homes for one or a number of reasons, including prolonged drought, soil erosion, disease, or conflict among the Anasazi themselves or with outsiders. The most famous Anasazi sites are Mesa Verde, Chaco Canyon, Canyon de Chelly, Pueblo Bonito, and Kayenta.

The Pueblo people possessed elaborate, formal ceremonials based upon a tradition of sacred myths. Most dances are dramatized prayers with participants dressed as divine spirits. Some impersonate kachinas, or animal spirits, who act as intermediaries between people and their gods. Through such rituals the Pueblos prayed for rain, crops, sunlight, and fertility. These traditions survived Spanish conquest, revolution, and pressure to convert to Christianity.

Although many Pueblo villages were established after initial Spanish contact, most are located close to earlier sites that were occupied before the people accepted a veneer of Catholicism. From the Spaniards they adopted horses, wheat, fruit trees, sheep, and cattle. The use of adobe bricks made from molds to rebuild larger rooms

TRIBAL NAMES

Achumawi	"river people"	Pecos	self-designation
Acoma	"person of"	Picuris	Spanish form of native term
Apache	"enemy"	Pima	"no"
Chimariko	"person"	Pojoaque	"drink water"
Chiricahua Apache	"great mountain"	Pomo	"village"
Coahuiltecan	Mexican place name	Pueblo	Spanish – "village," "town"
Cochiti	self-designation, i.e. "person of"	Sandia	Spanish – "watermelon"
Cocopa	Spanish form of native term	Seri	Spanish form of native term
Costanoan	Spanish – "coast people"	Serrano	Spanish – "mountaineers"
Cupeño	place name	Taos	"in the village"
Diegueño	Spanish mission name	Tesuque	"structure at a narrow place"
Gabrielino	Spanish mission name	Tonkawa	"they all stay together"
Havasupai	"blue water people"	Tubatulabal	"pine nut eaters"
Hopi	"peaceful ones"	Walapai	"pine tree folk"
Jemez	self-designation	Wappo	Spanish – "brave," "fine" or
Jicarilla Apache	Spanish – "little basket"		"handsome"
Karok	"upstream"	Washoe	"person"
Kawaiisu	"people"	Wintun	"people"
Kitanemuk	"house"	Wiyot	district name
Lipan Apache	"people"	Yana	"person"
Luiseño-Juaneño	Spanish mission names	Yavapai	"people of the sun"
Maidu	"person"	Yokuts	"person"
Mescalero Apache	Spanish – "mescal people"	Yuki	"stranger"
Miwok	"people"	Yuma	Spanish form of native term
Mohave	"three mountains" (possibly)	Yurok	"downstream"
Nambe	"earth"	Zia	"person of"
Navajo	area name	Zuñi	Spanish form of native term
Papago	"bean people"		

Names with no known meaning
Atsugewi, Chumash, Esselen, Hano, Kamia, Kiowa Apache, Maricopa, Piro, Shasta, Tigua, Towa.

Spanish names
Cahuilla, Laguna, Isleta, Salina, San Felipe, San Ildefonso, San Juan, Santa Ana, Santa Clara, Santo Domingo

in the Pueblo structures was also of Spanish origin. From the early 1700s until the U.S. annexation of the Southwest in 1848, the Pueblos and Spanish (and Mexicans, after the 1820s) stood back to back fighting off the Athabascans, who had first appeared in the fifteenth century. Although warfare between the Navajo and Apache and the Pueblo and Spanish often reached alarming proportions, the northern raiders still adopted weaving, pottery, masked dances, and even some agriculture from the Pueblos. The Athabascans retained their roving, hunting, and raiding northern ways, however; hardy, skilled in combat, incredibly observant, and gifted at concealment, they were very effective as warriors.

Of all Indian cultures, those of the Southwest have succeeded as much as any at maintaining their cultural identity. Despite the merging of Anglo-American material culture with their own, they have kept a strong attachment to the well-supported old religion and ceremonials, from which non-Natives are often excluded.

Above: **In the 1800s, Apaches lived in brush wickiups like this one, with Plains-style tipis the housing choice of the Mescalero, Lipan, and Jicarilla tribes. By 2000, the large majority of homes on reservations were single family houses valued at less than $50,000, many without telephone service and heated by wood or propane gas.**

The southwestern division of the Athabascan linguistic family comprised seven tribes: the Chiricahua, Jicarilla, Kiowa Apache, Lipan, Mescalero, Western Apache, and Navajo (Navaho). All but the Kiowa Apache language seem to be closely related branches of a single language that were perhaps not separate before about A.D. 1300. There has been lengthy debate over the route taken by these Athabascans following their separation from their northern relatives in the Mackenzie River drainage of Canada. The currently favored theory suggests a migration through the Plateau and Great Basin. A second view suggests a route through the Great Plains—and credits these Apacheans as the first Great Plains people to be in contact with the earliest Spanish exploration of the Plains in the sixteenth and seventeenth centuries. A number of archaeological sites such as Dismal River and others in Nebraska and Kansas may be Apachean, although some historians consider them more probably Puebloan. In the course of the debate, a number of tribal names in old Spanish and French records have been given Apache status, including the Padouca—but they may instead be Comanche, a relatively recent Plains people. In any case, the Apacheans began entering the Southwest from about A.D. 1400, with the Kiowa Apache and then the Lipan diverging to the plains of Oklahoma and Texas.

A number of Indian groups of northern Mexico, such as the Manso, Suma, Jumano, and Janos—names known from old Spanish mission records—have also been presented as Apachean, but none survived until the late nineteenth century, so their connections are unknown.

CHIRICAHUA APACHE
A tribe of the southwestern Apachean group who lived on the west side of the Rio Grande in southwestern New Mexico and adjacent Arizona and Mexico. Although they had almost no tribal cohesion, they are sometimes divided into four bands: Chiricahua,

Mimbreños, Mogollon, and Warm Springs. Their closest linguistic relatives are the Mescalero Apache. By 1853, most of the Chiricahua territory had been transferred from Mexico to the United States, but hostilities continued between miners, ranchers, settlers, and these nomadic Indians. The U.S. government made several attempts to settle some Chiricahua on reservations through overtures to leaders Mangas Coloradas and Cochise; when these failed, some were interned on the San Carlos Reservation. Thus began a long, dramatic, and tragic fight between a few hundred Apaches and the troops, scouts, and citizens of the United States and Mexico.

The Chiricahua leader Victorio and most of his followers were killed by Mexican soldiers in 1880, and not until 1886 did leader Geronimo and his band finally surrender to Gen. Nelson Miles in the Peloncillo Mountains' Skeleton Canyon, in the southeast corner of Arizona. The entire Chiricahua people were sent first to Florida and then to Alabama, but in 1894 they were transferred to Fort Sill, Oklahoma. In 1913, 187 of the remaining Chiricahua returned to their homelands and settled on the Mescalero Reservation, New Mexico, while 84 chose to remain in Oklahoma. The Oklahoma branch have descendants near Apache and Fletcher who are known as the "Fort Sill Apache."

Since then, the Chiricahua have all but merged with the Mescalero. However, 500 still claimed Chiricahua descent in 1970, and by 2000 there were 1,134 people who considered themselves solely Chiricahua. An additional 1,055 were part Chiricahua. Of the total, 730 lived in California, 216 in Texas, 86 in Arizona, 68 in New Mexico, and 48 in Oklahoma. By 2000 there were 253 Fort Sill Apache and an additional 58 who were part Fort Sill Apache. There were 153 in Oklahoma, 25 in California, and 19 in Texas.

JICARILLA APACHE (Tinde)

A tribe of the southwestern Athabascans closest to the Lipan in language. They call themselves *Tinde;* the term "Jicarilla" is derived from the Spanish and means "little basket." Their territory has historically

Below: **Essa-questa (Daha)— Kiowa Apache, c. 1870, holding a bow and wearing a bow-quiver case and beaded pouch.**

Above: **Apache Mountain Spirit Dancer, c. 1930.** Also called Gaan Dancers, they impersonate the sacred spirits who drive away sickness and evil and bring good fortune. Over black buckskin hoods with eyes of abalone or turquoise, they wear towering wooden headdresses painted with symbols of strength. They challenge the forces of evil by charging at each other in the dark beside a fire.

been the high country of mesas and basins in northern New Mexico on both sides of the Rio Grande and the upper valleys of the Red River; their hunting territory extended into present Colorado. Their location enabled them to hunt bison as well as antelope and small game, and they also gathered wild berries and fruits. Their early use of the horse and relative proximity to Plains Indians allowed the adoption of cultural traits and material culture from the east and north. Like other Apaches, the Jicarilla raided the Pueblos extensively and also incorporated both ritual and material culture from Pueblo people; they were the Apaches most influenced by Pueblo agriculture. They probably encountered the Spanish in the sixteenth century and thereafter were engaged in frequent conflict with them. The Jicarilla were, in turn, harassed by the Comanche during the eighteenth century, and hostilities with the settlers and the U.S. government continued until 1855.

In 1874, the Jicarilla Reservation was established near Tierra Amarilla, New Mexico, but they were moved several times between 1878 and 1887. The present reservation centered at Dulce, New Mexico, has been their home since 1887 and was substantially expanded in 1908.

Their major ceremonials were the Bear Dance, a curing rite; and the Relay Race between two sides, enlisting the aid of culture heroes and deities to ensure a plentiful food supply. The Jicarilla have retained a surprising amount of traditional religion and beliefs despite modern influences but do not have the Mountain Spirit rituals of the Western Apache (see left).

Their population was 815 in 1900, about the same as in 1845, and has grown steadily since. In 1980, there were 2,308 Jicarillas and in 2000, 3,132. An additional 368 were reported as part Jicarilla. Of the total, 161 lived in California, 92 in Arizona, and 56 in Texas. The largest number, 2,729, lived in New Mexico, mostly on the 750,000-acre (303,525-hectare) Jicarilla Reservation in the northwestern part of the state near the Colorado border.

The Jicarilla Reservation is one of the leading oil and gas producing reservations in the United States, and the Jicarilla were the first tribe in the United States to own 100 percent of the wells located on their reservation. The reservation is also world-renowned for hunting and fishing, and its 14,500-acre (5,900-ha) Horse Lake Mesa Game Park is the largest single elk preserve in the country. Annual events on the reservation include the Little Beaver Roundup, held in July, and the Go-Jii-Yah Feast in September.

Above: **Mescalero Apache Crown Dancers. Masked and painted dancers representing Mountain Spirits (Gaans) appear during girls' puberty ceremonies. Their elaborately painted head boards and bodies enshrine symbolism for well-being, connecting the dancers with the supernatural world. This photograph was taken at Ruidoso, Mescalero Reservation, New Mexico, c. 1947.**

KIOWA APACHE

The most divergent group of the southwestern Apachean people. Associated with the Kiowa of the southern Plains since long before white contact, perhaps for four hundred years, this Apachean people may have moved from the north with their allies the Kiowa and not separated from the main southern group, as has been believed. Superficially, they are a Plains people who formed a distinct band within their adopted tribe. They actively acquired and traded horses for the Northern Plains tribes. In the 1860s, they moved to the Fort Sill Reservation in Oklahoma, along with Kiowa and Comanche. In 1907, they were reported to number 156. In 1960, they were living in and about the towns of Anadarko, Fort Cobb, and Apache in Oklahoma and numbered about 400, including about 40 who could speak their language. In 1981, their population reached 833, with only 20 still speaking the language. By 2000, the Kiowa Apache were no longer a federally recognized tribe.

Below: **Apache Indians at Gallup, New Mexico, c. 1910. Several are dressed to represent the Mountain Spirits or Gaans, wearing masks of black hoods with attached split yucca laths painted with mythological and sacred designs. Photograph J. R. Willis.**

LIPAN APACHE (Tindi)

An Athabascan tribe of the southwestern Apachean group who lived in the upper Red River area of northwestern Texas as long ago as 1670. At that time, they numbered perhaps 3,000 and already had horses and metal weapons. They seem to have pushed eastward several Caddoan peoples who were subsequently armed by the French. This, in turn, halted and reversed the Lipan advance. They apparently played a large part in destroying Spanish settlements and missions in the San Antonio area, but the entry of the Comanche into Texas diminished their numbers and domain. In later years they lived between the Colorado and Pecos Rivers in Texas. A few crossed into Mexico. Their language was closest to that of the Jicarilla, whom they perhaps split from in about 1500.

The last of the Lipan were settled in 1905 on the Mescalero Reservation, in New Mexico; there were only two or three old women living in 1981 who knew anything of their ancient language. A few others are said to have been integrated among the Kiowa Apache and Tonkawa of Oklahoma but are no longer reported separately. The Lipan, together with the Mescalero and Tonkawa, are thought to have been the spreaders of Peyote use among Indians

north of Mexico. By 2000, there were only 131 people who identified themselves solely as Lipan Apache and 77 who were part Lipan. Of the overall total, 110 lived in Texas and 5 in New Mexico.

MESCALERO APACHE

A branch of the southwestern Athabascan Apachean peoples that has occupied essentially the same territory of Texas, southeastern New Mexico, and adjacent parts of Chihuahua, Mexico, since the seventeenth century. Today, they are the third largest Apache group. Their territory combined high mountain valleys and flats with cold winters and hot, dry summers. Despite treaties with the Spanish and later Mexican authorities, when Texas and New Mexico were transferred to the United States, the new government recognized no Indian land claims. A bitter struggle between Americans and Mescaleros saw many taken prisoner at Bosque Redondo on the Pecos River along with the Navajos. In 1872, a reservation was established in Otero County, New Mexico. The Mescalero, with some Chiricahua and Lipans, have been there ever since.

Above: **An Apache woman doing beadwork, c. 1950. Some Apache bands, particularly those closest to the Plains tribes, such as the Jicarilla and Mescalero, excelled in beadwork. The cradleboard with its sun shade and yucca slats resembles those of Apache relatives, the Navajo.**

Like most Apaches, the Mescalero lived by hunting wild game, antelope, rabbit, and occasionally buffalo, and harvesting wild plants, particularly agave (mescal), prickly pear, wild pea, berries, and chokecherries. The Apaches were expert basket makers; they wore buckskin clothing; their house types were brush wickiups and, among the Mescalero, Lipan, and Jicarilla, Plains-style tipis.

The Apaches revered two powerful supernaturals, Child of the Water and his mother, White Painted Woman. Two important observances are the girls' puberty rite and the Mountain Spirit (Gaans) Dances, which were held to protect the Apache from hostile forces and epidemic disease and involved masked dancers with distinctive hoods and headdresses.

The Mescalero numbered perhaps 2,000 in 1850, but only 431 in 1888, 868 in 1945, and 1,300 in 1980, although the last two figures include the mixed Mescalero-Chiricahua population. By 2000, there were 5,374 people who were solely Mescalero and an additional 1,653 who were part Mescalero. Of the total, 3,180 lived in New Mexico, 1,572 in California, 533 in Texas, and 147 in Arizona.

The majority of Mescalero tribal members live on the 460,661-acre (186,429-ha) Mescalero Reservation, in New Mexico. Annual reservation events include the Mescalero Apache Maiden festival and Mountain Spirit Dances, held in July, which also include a professional Indian rodeo. Significant tribal business ventures include Ski Apache, one of the largest ski resorts in the Southwest. They also own and operate the Inn of the Mountain Gods, a luxury hotel and resort complex with a golf course and a casino.

The Mescalero tribal government consists of a self-governing, eight-member Tribal Council. The council has an elected president and vice president. Officials serve a two-year term. The four council members elected each year by secret ballot approve fiscal matters and policies for operations, law and order, and business enterprises.

Below: **A Jicarilla Apache group, 1904. Although the clothing of this tribe was Plains-influenced, there were many purely Jicarilla traits: for example, the women's broad, tacked leather belts, woolen hair ties, and the style of dress yoke shown at right.**

WESTERN APACHE
A group of Athabascan subtribes speaking similar dialects, in southeastern Arizona from the San Pedro River in the south to the Verde River in the north, and comprising the San Carlos, White Mountain, Cibecue, Southern Tonto, and Northern Tonto in that order south to north. They have become one of the legendary Indian peoples due to

their prowess as warriors and have been fancifully depicted in popular fiction.

They probably reached their present location in about A.D. 1525 and remained isolated until hostilities with the Spanish intensified after 1765. The Apache adoption of the horse and the material culture of equestrian raiders ensured their independence until the United States obtained control of Arizona in 1853. U.S. efforts to destroy the Apaches intensified with the concentration of Western Apaches on the San Carlos Reservation, established in 1872 in eastern Arizona south of the Colorado Plateau (San Carlos and Tonto), and the Fort Apache Reservation to the north (White Mountain and Cibecue).

The Western Apache worldview was expressed in a cycle of myths that explained the origin of the world and supernatural powers. Their major ceremonials were connected with curing or protection against illness, usually performed in special structures. Traditional Apaches have a belief in an impersonal deity, "Life Giver," and culture heroes "Changing Woman" and her son "Slayer of Monsters." The Apache puberty ceremony survives, and Gaan or Crown dancers (Mountain Spirit Dances) continue to perform regularly.

In Census 2000, 68 percent of all Apaches who identified themselves as belonging to a specific Apache subgroup were members of one of the three recognized Western Apache tribes. The largest of these is the White Mountain Apache, with a population of 12,107, plus an additional 497 people who identify themselves as having partial ancestry. Next is the San Carlos Apache, numbering 9,716, plus 363 who are part San Carlos Apache. The smallest group is the Payson Tonto Apache, with a population of 131, plus 56 of mixed descent. Most Western Apache live in Arizona—virtually 100 percent of the Tonto and 92 percent of both the White Mountain and San Carlos people. Nearly all of the tribal members residing in Arizona live on or near the reservations discussed below.

Above: **Western Apache, c. 1860. Perhaps the hardiest of all Native American warriors, a few hundred Apaches defied other tribes, Mexicans, and the U.S. Army until the 1880s. Although often depicted wearing much Euro-American clothing, they had their own distinctive dress. Buckskin shirts with cut or applied fringing were decorated with yellow ocher and lines of beadwork and silver buttons. Warrior and ceremonial buckskin caps bore eagle, turkey, ibis, or owl feathers. Calf-length moccasins with rawhide soles extended at the toe were often painted and beaded in lines. Rawhide shields were invested with great protective and concealing powers by painted black, yellow, green, and white designs of stars, crescent moons, the Sun, birds, bats, and spirit forms, often split into cardinal sections or groups of four elements.**

The White Mountain Apache Tribe lives on the 1.6-million-acre (647,520-ha) Fort Apache Reservation, established in 1891. It is located in the east central part of Arizona, about 200 miles (320 kilometers) northeast of Phoenix. The roughly 12,000 tribal members on the reservation live in nine major communities, of which Whiteriver, the capital, is the largest with 2,500 citizens. The Tribal Council consists of the tribal chairman, vice chairman, and nine council members elected from four separate districts. Council members are elected to a four-year term. They represent the tribe and its people in matters that concern the welfare of the tribe and exercise all powers vested in the tribe through its inherent sovereignty.

Established in 1969, the White Mountain Apache Cultural Center is located on the 288-acre (117-ha) site of the former U.S. Army post at Fort Apache. The Apache Office of Tourism is located in the 1870 building at the fort that was occupied by General Crook during the Apache Wars of the late nineteenth century. The Cultural Center now serves as a repository for tribal cultural heritage, preserving oral histories, archival materials, and objects of cultural, historical, and artistic significance.

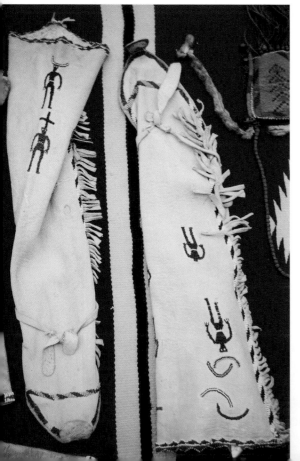

Below: **Apache buckskin boots, with beadwork representing the Gaan (Mountain Spirits), c. 1900.**

The major employment on the Fort Apache Reservation includes a timber mill and a remanufacturing plant, as well as recreation. The latter includes outdoor activities such as hunting and fishing, which are widely promoted on the reservation. For example, the tribe operates a fishing camp at Christmas Tree Lake. The tribe's Sunrise Park Resort is one of Arizona's leading skiing destinations, with summer and winter activities. The White Mountain Apache also operate the Hon-Dah Resort Casino and Conference Center in the reservation community of Pinetop, Arizona.

The San Carlos Apache Tribe occupies the 1.8-million-acre (728,460-ha) reservation of the same name in southeastern Arizona, established in 1871. With its capital in San

Carlos, the reservation is separated from the Fort Apache Indian Reservation to the north by the Black and Salt Rivers. Forest covers over one-third of the reservation, and one section contains part of the largest stand of ponderosa pine in the world. Many tribal members work in the forestry industry, although the largest employers are federal and state governmental agencies, which maintain offices on San Carlos land. In addition, cattle ranching contributes about a million dollars annually to the tribal economy. Another important aspect of the economy is recreation, which centers on San Carlos Lake. The San Carlos Apache also operate the Apache Gold Hotel and Casino, 7 miles (11 km) east of the Arizona city of Globe. The hotel complex, opened in 1994, also includes an eighteen-hole golf course. The San Carlos Apache Cultural Center was opened in 1995 in the town of Peridot on the reservation. A special exhibit, "Window on Apache Culture," describes the Apaches' spiritual beginnings and rituals such as the Changing Women Ceremony.

The Tonto Apache Reservation is in Gila County, Arizona, near the town of Payson, hence the official tribal name of Payson Tonto Apache. Payson, originally called Te-go-suk, or "Place of the Yellow Water," is approximately 95 miles (150 km) northeast of Phoenix and 100 miles (160 km) southeast of Flagstaff. Established in 1972, the 85-acre (34-ha) reservation is the smallest and newest of the Apache reservations. The Tonto Apache are the direct descendants of the Tontos who lived in the area prior to the nineteenth century. The tribe opened its Mazatzal Casino on the reservation in 1994.

Above: **A Jicarilla Apache buckskin shirt with beaded shoulder and arm strips, c. 1890.**

Below: **Nisenan, c. 1870. A Southern Maidu boy wearing "flicker feather" headdress across his forehead, large abalone shell gorget, and bandolier covered with abalone pendants and beads. Abalone objects were considered great wealth among the Maidu tribes.**

Three tribes related by their similar Penutian dialects. With a traditional homeland in the Sierra Nevada foothills and the inland mountain ranges of north central California, the three tribes are the Maidu proper, who traditionally occupied the upper reaches of the Feather River south of Eagle Lake around Susanville, Butte Valley, and Quincy; the Konkow, who lived on the east side of the Sacramento River around Chico; and the Southern Maidu or Nisenan, who occupied the Yuba, Bear, and American river valleys around Marysville, Nevada City, Placerville, and Auburn. The Maidu were participants in the important Kuksu religion of the Sacramento Valley, with its wide variety of rituals, impersonations of spirits, distinctive attire, and use of large semi-subterranean dance houses. They used bark or brush lean-to house structures and had an elaborate system of shell money exchange between mourners and their friends. To honor the dead, they burned property at funeral rites, including fine baskets made especially to be consumed in this way. Clothing was scant; they often wore aprons or breechcloths of buckskin.

Spanish contact was limited to the Nisenan, but American and Hudson's Bay trappers appeared in the 1820s, and after the Gold Rush the invasion of Maidu territory by white settlers (around 1849) upset the ecological balance. The Natives killed livestock and were then killed themselves in retribution. From a population of 9,000 in 1846, only about 1,100 were reported to survive in 1910—mostly Maidu in Plumas County, Konkow in Butte County, and Nisenan in Yuba, Placer, and El Dorado counties. Despite the economic disadvantages affecting most modern Californian Native descendants, there is a

heartening renewed interest in Maidu cultural
and traditional values, including the continuation
of the Maidu Bear Dance each spring at Janesville.

In Census 2000, there were 2,368 people who
identified themselves as Maidu and 1,727 who
considered themselves part Maidu. Of the former,
82 percent live in California, while 75 percent of
those with partial Maidu ancestry live in the state.
Today, most Maidu people identify themselves
simply as "Maidu." In 2000, there were only 26
Maidu who considered themselves Nisenan or part
Nisenan. The Konkow, or Konkow-Maidu, had 105
tribal members who were associated with the
Mooretown Rancheria near Oroville.

The Konkow-Maidu are descendants of ancient
northwestern Maidu who migrated to the Butte
County area in about 1200 B.C., settling on
Mooretown Ridge between the Middle Fork and
South Fork of the Feather River. Removed from
the area after the Gold Rush, they were allowed
to return to a rancheria near Mooretown in 1894.
This rancheria was officially disbanded in 1961, but
in 1979, a Pomo woman named Tillie Hardwicke
and six plaintiffs filed a class action suit on behalf
of thirty-four terminated rancherias, including
Mooretown. In 1983, Mooretown was among
seventeen that were reinstated and restored to
federally recognized status. Additional land,
including 35 acres (14 ha) south of Oroville,
was purchased in the 1980s and 1990s. Since
1997, there has been a major effort to restore
the original Konkow-Maidu dialect by teaching
it to tribal members.

Meanwhile, a second group of Konkow, calling
themselves the Konkow Valley Band, is seeking
federal recognition as being a distinct Maidu
subgroup. Now based in Oroville, they are
descended from Maidu who were forced, along
with members of several other tribes, onto the
Round Valley Reservation in Mendocino County
in the 1860s.

CALIFORNIA RANCHERIA

Including the Mooretown
Rancheria, there are five
California rancherias (small
reservations) that are recognized
today as distinct Maidu
subtribes, and there are several
others, including the Konkow
Valley people, working to obtain
federally recognized status. The
other four are the Berry Creek
Rancheria, with 129 members
identified as Tyme-Maidu; the
Enterprise Rancheria near
Oroville, with 40 members
identified as Estom-Yumeka-
Maidu; the Greenville Rancheria
near Redding, with 37 members;
and the Mechoopda Indian Tribe
of the Chico Rancheria, with a
membership of 179. In each
case, well over half of the
members consider themselves
solely Maidu. In general, the
economic base involves
employment in the local
community, although casinos
are owned and operated by
the rancherias at Mooretown
and Berry Creek.

A large group of Indians forming a Penutian linguistic family in northern and central California, comprising the main body of the family, the Valley (Eastern) Miwok, and two small detached groups, the Coast Miwok and Lake Miwok. The Coast Miwok lived north of San Francisco Bay, mainly around Tomales Bay and Point Reyes, but ranging north to Duncan's Point and east to Sonoma Creek. The Lake Miwok lived farther north and inland, mainly in the Clear Lake basin. The Valley Miwok lived along the western slopes of the Sierra Nevada from the Sacramento and San Joaquin deltas south to the Fresno River. Major Miwok-related archaeological sites have been discovered in and around Yosemite National Park. All three separate groups were semi-sedentary hunter/gatherers. The nearly two hundred archaeological sites that have been discovered give an indication of the relative size of the three groups. Of these, 65 percent are Valley Miwok sites and 26 percent are Coast Miwok sites.

In 1579, the Coast Miwok became the first Miwok to have contact with Europeans, when Sir Francis Drake landed and wintered at Point Reyes. According to baptismal records, the Miwoks had contact with Spanish missionaries in San Francisco by 1811, and possibly as early as 1776.

Anthropologist Alfred Kroeber

Below: **Miwok boys, c. 1960, wearing traditional ceremonial dress, including headbands of flicker feathers, in front of a roundhouse in Tuolumne County, California. These boys were part of a cultural group reviving Californian Indian traditions.**

estimates that the Miwok population stood at around 9,000 in 1770, although other estimates suggest as many as 15,000. A malaria epidemic in 1833 is known to have killed a substantial number of Miwoks. The Valley Miwok were at war sporadically with Spanish settlers in the early nineteenth century, and in 1837, roughly 100 were killed in a battle with the settlers. The Gold Rush of 1849 brought a major encroachment of white settlers and prospectors into the Sierra Nevada. The Valley Miwok under Chief Tenaya struck back in 1851 in what was called the Mariposa Indian War.

In the early twentieth century, small reservations or rancherias were established, and some Miwok descendants still live on these. The Miwok population was given as 670 in 1910 and 763 in 1930. By 2000, there were 80 people who considered themselves Coast Miwok and another 87 who were part Coast Miwok. Of the total, 77 percent lived in California. Meanwhile, there were 110 people who described themselves as Miwok, 82 of them associated with a band centered at Ione and 28 associated with the band at Shingle Springs. There were also 67 people who were part Miwok.

The majority of the people are now known as Me-Wuk. According to Census 2000, there were 2,881 who were solely Me-Wuk and 2,491 who were part Me-Wuk. Only a handful of these were associated with a specific rancheria. The Jackson Rancheria had 37 members, but only 4 in California. The Tuolumne Band of Me-Wuk had 29, of which 24 lived in the state. During the 1990s, both the Tuolumne Band and the Jackson Rancheria opened casinos on their land. Three other federally recognized Me-Wuk rancherias had fewer than a dozen members at the turn of the century. These were the Buena Vista Rancheria, the Chicken Ranch Rancheria, and the Sheep Ranch Rancheria.

Above: **A Miwok shelter made from strips of wood and bark.**

Above: **A Papago woman cleaning wheat by the age-old method of winnowing (tossing in the air allowing the heavier wheat to be separated from the lighter chaff).**

Below: **Early twentieth century photograph of a Pima woman.**

Descendants of the Hohokam people and related through a similar Uto-Aztecan language. The Papago now refer to themselves as the Tohono O'odham, which means "Desert People." The Pima, meanwhile, are known as the Akimel Au-authm, meaning "River People." The Pima are also associated with a third tribe, the Yuman-speaking Maricopa, who are known as Xalychidom Pipaash, "People who live toward the water." Whereas the Hohokam and their descendants have lived in central Arizona for centuries, the Maricopa have been in the area only for about two hundred years.

The Pima and the Papago historically occupied an area of the Sonoran Desert that is now part of southern Arizona and northern Sonora, Mexico. The extensive range of Pima and Papago villages was generally south of the Gila River to the Rio Magdalena, Mexico. Before the arrival of the Spanish in the mid-seventeenth century, the tribes were part of a desert food-collecting culture that adopted the successful farming of domesticated plants, including corn, beans, and squash. This agriculture, of Mesoamerican origin, was developed by the Hohokam people, who skillfully built canals to lead river or arroyo water to their fields. The Hohokam disappeared in about A.D. 1400. Maintaining a sufficient water supply was the major concern of the Pimas, so larger communities were established along the San Pedro and Santa Cruz Rivers where a subtribe, the Sobaipuri, were located.

The Spanish brought livestock, wheat, and improved implements for canal and ditch irrigation. They also converted the Pima-Papago population to nominal Catholicism through the establishment of missions. The Americans came after 1854, and, although they exerted control over the territory, there was little settlement pressure and relations were generally good. While tribal fortunes reached a low point around 1900, on the whole the Pima have adapted to an Indian-Hispanic-Anglo culture.

In Census 2000, 8,519 people were reported as Pima and 2,974 part Pima. Of these, 76 percent and 50 percent, respectively, lived in Arizona, home of the two Pima reservations, Gila River and Salt River. There were also 17,466 Tohono O'odham people and 2,621 part Tohono O'odham. The percentage of those living in Arizona were 88 and 50, respectively.

The Ak-Chin Indian Community in the Santa Cruz Valley, south of Phoenix, includes both Tohono O'odham and Pima. It is located 43 miles (69 km) west of the Casa Grande Ruins National Monument, a Hohokam archaeological site from the thirteenth century. Established in May 1912, the reservation was reduced from 47,600 acres (19,260 ha) to just under 22,000 acres (8,900 ha) four months later. Agriculture is possible on 15,000 acres (6,070 ha) under irrigation, but water is scarce. In 1984, the tribe was granted access to additional Colorado River water. Other economic development has included an industrial park with railroad access and the Harrah's Phoenix Ak-Chin Casino. The Him-Dak Museum at the reservation displays tribal crafts.

The 52,600-acre (21,287-ha) Salt River Indian Community, northeast of Phoenix, is home to nearly 6,000 Pima and Maricopa. Created in 1879, it maintains 19,000 acres (7,690 ha) in their natural state, with agriculture as a secondary land use. Crops include cotton, melons, potatoes, onions, and carrots. Due to the reservation's proximity to the upscale Phoenix suburb of Scottsdale, there is substantial retail development on Pima Road at one corner of the tribal land. The tribe also operates two casinos nearby.

The Tohono O'odham Nation consists of four smaller, disconnected Papago Indian reservations totaling 2.8 million acres (1.13 million ha)—roughly the size of Connecticut. The largest community, Sells, functions as the nation's capital. Its economic base includes a sprawling industrial park near Tucson that contains a 23-acre (9-ha) foreign trade zone and major operations of the Caterpillar tractor company. The Desert Diamond Casino in Tucson opened in 1993, followed by the smaller Golden Hasan Casino in 1999.

GILA RIVER RESERVATION

The 372,000-acre (150,550-ha) Gila River Indian Reservation is located south of Phoenix. It was established by an act of Congress in 1859 and its constitution was formally established in 1939. The Pima tribal administrative offices and departments are located in Sacaton. The reservation continues to develop its industrial, agricultural, retail, and recreational economic base. There are 15,000 acres (6,070 ha) of tribal-owned farms, producing crops such as cotton, wheat, millet, alfalfa, barley, melons, pistachios, olives, citrus, and vegetables. Independent farming operations cultivate an additional 22,000 acres (8,900 ha) of similar crops. The community currently operates three industrial parks that are home to several local and national companies. One park, Lone Butte Industrial Park, is nationally acclaimed as one of the most successful Indian industrial parks in the United States. On the recreational side, a substantial golf and resort complex opened in October 2002. It includes two world-class eighteen-hole golf courses and a five-hundred-room hotel resort complex. The reservation community operates two casinos, the Wild Horse Pass south of Chandler and the Vee Quiva on the west side of Phoenix. The reservation also contains the Gila River Arts and Crafts Center and the Gila River Heritage Theme Park.

An important group of seven related tribes speaking differing dialects forming a family of the Hokan stock in California centered around Clear Lake and along the coast from Fort Bragg in the north to beyond Stewarts Point in the south in Mendocino, Lake, and Sonoma Counties. They were a populous people, numbering over 14,000 in the eighteenth century. In the mild climate the Pomos used little clothing; in cool weather they wore mantles, capes, robes, and skirts of vegetable fiber or skins. They hunted rabbits, deer, sea mammals, and bears with bows and arrows, heavy spears, nets, and snares. They had ample supplies of fish.

The Pomo lived in conical huts of redwood bark or planks, and around Clear Lake houses were built of bunches of tule or coarse-textured grass. They are also known for the excellent quality of their baskets, which survive in abundance in museums. The social core of Pomo life was the family and the small village; their beliefs were part of a religious system called the Kuksu, which stressed curing rituals and elaborate forms of dancing and fire-eating to ensure the absence of danger from ghosts.

The Russians established a settlement at Fort Ross in 1811; but the Mexicans made the first serious inroads into Pomo life and culture in the 1820s and 1830s, taking lands and introducing cholera and smallpox. Land loss continued during expansion and settlement by the United States, and the Pomo ultimately became almost without land in their own country, working on the ranches and farms of white settlers. They did, however, reestablish small settlements in the late nineteenth century, and a number of small reservations or rancherias were established.

A revitalization movement, the Bole-Maru religion, still survives alongside the Pomo branch of the Methodist Church. In 1958, under the Rancheria Termination Act, a number of the Pomo rancherias ceased to exist, and administration of the

Below: **Pomo balsas. A canoe-shaped raft of tied reed (tule) used by fishermen on Clear Lake and its swampy environs, but unsuitable for ocean mammal hunting.**

remaining rancherias was to be transferred from federal to state jurisdiction. The law called for tribes to vote on a plan to divide communal tribal property into parcels that would be owned by individual tribal members. Under this scheme, twenty-three rancherias statewide ceased to exist as federally recognized tribes by 1970. In the ensuing years, a number of Pomo bands sought to reinstate their federal status. Tillie Hardwicke, a member of the Pinoleville Pomo in Mendocino County, brought a class action lawsuit against the U.S. government on behalf of seventeen terminated rancherias. She won, and in December 1983, the government restored federal recognition to the reservations and their tribal governments.

In Census 2000, there were 5,111 people who considered themselves solely Pomo, up from 2,626 in 1970 and 4,766 in 1990. In addition, there were 2,763 with partial Pomo ancestry in 2000. Ninety-one percent of the Pomo and 83 percent of those of mixed descent lived within California. Of these, only a small number were associated with the eighteen Pomo rancherias in the state.

The largest Pomo communities are the Sherwood Valley Rancheria with 237 members, the Stewarts Point Rancheria (Kashaya Band) with 228 members, the Hopland Rancheria with 215 members, the Dry Creek Rancheria with 153 members, the Manchester–Point Arena Rancheria with 140 members, and the Robinson Rancheria with 139.

The smaller Pomo rancherias were the Scotts Valley Band, the Stonyford Rancheria, the Elem Indian Colony of the Sulphur Bank, the Guidiville Rancheria, the Lytton Rancheria, the Cloverdale Rancheria, the Coyote Valley Band, the Middletown Rancheria, the Pinoleville Rancheria, the Potter Valley Rancheria, the Redwood Valley Rancheria, and the Upper Lake Rancheria. There were also a handful of Pomo present on the Big Valley Rancheria of Pomo and Pit River Indians. The Sherwood Valley, Dry Creek, Coyote Valley, Hopland, and Middletown rancherias all operate casinos.

Above: **Pomo man in Bole-Maru dress, c. 1925.**

Below: **A tribal casino sign.**

Above: **Navajo hunter, c. 1895. Navajo silverwork, employing Mexican techniques, perhaps dates only from the Navajos' return from imprisonment at Bosque Redondo (1868). At first Mexican coins were worked with simple metal tools, but by 1930, commercial blowtorches and solder were being used alongside files, saws, and punches. This hunter (note his fur and skin quiver/bow case slung over his right shoulder) wears a "squash blossom" necklace and a sand-cast *naja* pendant of supposed Islamic inspiration. His shoulder strap has a pouch for tobacco and small items and bears plain silver buttons; his belt conchos have embossed centers stamped from large dies, the sparse decoration hammered with chisels. Later, turquoise and more elaborate designs were introduced, spreading to the Zuñi and Hopi, and increasingly designed for sale to whites. However, good Navajo work retains its quality.**

One of the seven divisions of the southwestern Athabascan Apachean group (see Apache, page 12). After the Cherokee, the Navajo (or Navaho) are the second largest tribe in the United States according to census figures, but the largest under the BIA. They call themselves Diné and perhaps entered the American Southwest during the fifteenth century. Linguistically they are closest to the Western Apache. Their location was, and still is, the dry desert regions of northeastern Arizona and northwestern New Mexico, between the San Juan River in the north and the Puerco and San Jose Rivers in the south. The Navajo seem to have been more heavily influenced by Pueblo culture than other Apachean groups; Navajo pottery and weaving, for example, are of Pueblo origin.

Although the Navajo were involved in wars against the Spanish and were often successful in driving them away, their culture gradually modified under Spanish influence, including the domestication of sheep and horses. This influence also affected food gathering, agriculture, trade, religion, and the arts, leading to a hybrid Apachean-Puebloan-Hispanic tradition which survives among the Navajo to this day.

The Navajo origin myth describes the people ascending from the underworld. Their ceremonials are held primarily for curing disease, actual or anticipated. Navajo rituals seek to restore universal harmony once it has been disturbed, such as with the "Blessing Way," a traditional healing ceremony that respects the connection between people, spirit and nature. Other important rituals include the Yeibichei or "Night Chant." Recently the Native American Church has become popular with many Navajos.

After the United States obtained control of the Southwest, legendary government scout Kit Carson was commissioned to round up the Navajo, and in doing so he destroyed their sheep, orchards, food, and horses. Some 8,000 Navajo were interned at Bosque Redondo in New Mexico in 1863. They returned five years later, and the Navajo Reservation was established.

The 16-million-acre (6.5-million-ha) reservation straddles four states: Arizona, New Mexico, Utah, and Colorado. The fact that it completely surrounds the Hopi Reservation in Arizona has led to numerous jurisdictional disputes between the tribes. During the twentieth century, three additional communities have been added to the Navajo Reservation in New Mexico: at Ramah, in Cibola and McKinley Counties; Cañoncito, west of Albuquerque; and Puertocito, northwest of Magdalena, Socorro County.

Navajo life today centers on attempts to cope with the many economic and political problems that stem from their longtime cultural isolation, and to ensure that exploitation by various corporations of the mineral resources on their lands will benefit "The People" generally. The Navajos are noted for their fine silverwork, woolen blankets and rugs; and for their continued distinctive dress, particularly of the women, which is derived from nineteenth-century full skirts and long blouses of European fashion.

In 2000, there were 269,202 Navajos (see page 32), compared to 158,633 in 1980 and 225,298 in 1990. In addition, another 28,995 people consider themselves part Navajo. Forty-seven percent of Navajos live in Arizona and 38 percent live in New Mexico. Of those with partial Navajo ancestry, 20 percent live in Arizona and 16 percent live in New Mexico.

In terms of land area, the Navajo Nation has the largest reservation in the United States; it is larger than all of New England combined, excluding Maine. The Navajo Nation also has the country's largest tribal government body. The Navajo Tribal Council has eighty-eight members, elected every four years by popular vote by the Navajo people on and off the reservation. The tribe, like others, has the power of taxation and can tax non-Indians using tribal lands for farming and grazing. They also levy taxes on oil and gas extracted by non-Indian

Above: Sandpainting, c. 1950. Dry "paintings" serve as temporary altars during the various "ways" or healing rites, depicting supernatural beings in human or human-like forms, often in pairs or larger multiples. Yeibichai masked dancer spirit representations are often depicted during night-long curing rites and—unlike fixed sandpaintings for commercial sale—are always destroyed before dawn.

Below: **Mythological figures produced by finely ground colored sands on the floor of a hogan aided the Navajo in curing ceremonies. These paintings must be destroyed before sundown on the day they are prepared, or they will have no effect on patients.**

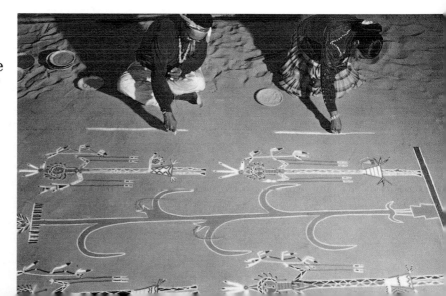

companies operating on the reservation. Federal law requires non-Navajo entities to obtain permits from the tribal government before they can open businesses on the reservation.

Navajo tribal courts decide civil disputes between Navajos and non-Navajos on the reservation, and deal with divorce, child custody problems, civil disputes between Navajo citizens, and minor crimes. Federal law enforcement handles major crimes such as murder, arson, burglary, and robbery. Court proceedings within the Navajo Nation are conducted in the Navajo language, in English, or in a mixture of both languages.

The city of Window Rock, Arizona (known as Ni' 'Alnii'gi, or "Earth's Center"), has been the capital and administrative center of the Navajo Nation since 1936. It takes its name from a hole in the 200-foot (61-meter) sandstone hill overlooking the city. Window Rock is the home of the Navajo Nation Council House and the Navajo Nation Museum. The Navajo Nation Fair is held annually at the Window Rock Fairgrounds.

The economy of the Navajo Nation includes lumbering, mining, and farming. The *Navajo Times* is the largest tribally-owned newspaper in the United States. Each week, the printed edition of the paper reaches more than 43,000 readers in North America, Europe, and Japan. An online edition is also available.

The Navajo Nation was the first tribe to operate its own educational system. Opening in 1966, the Rough Rock Demonstration School at Chinle, Arizona, was the first Indian-directed and Indian-controlled elementary school in the nation. In 1968, Navajo Community College (now Dine College) became the first Indian-owned and Indian-directed college.

Below: **A Navajo woman weaving a rug, c. 1950. The Navajo learned their weaving techniques from the Pueblo Indians, using wool from sheep introduced to the Southwest by the Spanish. Originally they used their own herds and native dyes for blankets; later they imported wools for rugs styled to non-Native tastes.**

The name of the so-called Pueblo Indians of the American Southwest, derived from the Spanish for "village," and a collective term for Indians who lived in permanent stone or adobe structures in compact villages along the Rio Grande in New Mexico, as well as the Zuñi of western New Mexico and the Hopi of northern Arizona. The historic Pueblos seem to be descendants of the Anasazi people, who built the great architectural wonders at Chaco Canyon, Mesa Verde, Casa Grande, and other places spread over five states, which were at the height of their cultural development in about the thirteenth century.

The Pueblos who survived the Spanish conquest are divided into four linguistic families: Tanoan, Keresan, Zuñi, and Hopi—the last a divergent branch of the old Shoshonean family, now called Uto-Aztecan. They were sedentary horticulturists who farmed intensively, usually in small fields irrigated from streams or storage reservoirs. Their chief crops were corn, pumpkins, melons, beans, and squash. They also raised a native cotton that was woven into everyday clothing. In addition to agriculture, they hunted deer and antelope, and bison on the plains. After contact with the Spanish, the Pueblos adopted horses, cattle, and sheep, and began to grow wheat, grapes, peaches, and apples. They domesticated turkeys, which were herded in large flocks, and kept eagles in captivity for their feathers, prized for ritual use.

Today, a number of the pueblo, or settlements, still survive. Most of these are located in the Rio Grande valley of northern New Mexico, north and west of Albuquerque. Each maintains an independent tribal identity, although culturally they are similar. The southern Pueblo languages are Keresan (Keres) and Tanoan, which incorporates the Tewa, Tiwa, and Towa dialects. These pueblos are the Keres-speaking Cochiti, San Felipe, Santa Ana, Santo Domingo, and Zia, who form the eastern group, and Acoma and Laguna, who form the western group. The Tanoan-speaking pueblos are Taos and Picuris (northern Tiwa); Sandia, Isleta, Tigua, and Piro (southern

Below: **A Hopi kachina. Usually made from cottonwood root and decorated with fur, leather, and turquoise, they are an important part of Hopi and Zuñi culture and provide a link with supernatural spirits.**

Tiwa); Nambe, San Ildefonso, San Juan, Santa Clara, Tesuque, Pojoaque (northern Tewa); Tano, now Hopi, Tewa (southern Tewa); Jemez and Pecos (Towa). Of these Piro and Pecos are no longer occupied, leaving 18 still inhabited. In addition to these eighteen tribal sites, a related site known as Ysleta del Sur is located within the city limits of El Paso, Texas, and is home to the Tewa-speaking Tigua people.

There are similar settlements occupied by the Zuñi and Hopi people, who differ linguistically from the Pueblo people. They are usually associated with the Pueblo because, unlike most other tribes anywhere on the continent, they have lived in permanent, well-constructed cities for more than a century. The Zuñi settlements are west of Albuquerque near the Arizona border, while the Hopi towns are on three mesas in northeastern Arizona, completely surrounded by the Navajo Nation.

The Zuñi seem to have been the first group the Spanish encountered, and reports of their "golden cities" inspired the Coronado expedition of 1540. Expecting to find great wealth, and encouraged always by news of what lay beyond, Francisco Vásquez de Coronado explored Pueblo country for two years without finding the hoped-for riches. It was not until 1598 that Juan de Oñate set up a permanent colony. What followed were vigorous Spanish attempts to "missionize," to suppress Native religion and

Below: **Corn dance, Santa Clara Pueblo, New Mexico.**

convert Indians to Christianity, and to enforce labor and tribute, which eventually led to the Pueblo Revolt of 1680, with the Spanish defeated and driven out.

It was not until 1696 that the Spanish regained control. They were thereafter less harsh in their treatment of the Indians, and the Pueblos continued in their ancient beliefs while adopting a veneer of Catholicism. Few Rio Grande Pueblos maintained their exact original sites after the Revolt; perhaps only Acoma and Isleta. Since then, the Pueblos have co-existed peacefully with whites, with a relatively stable culture that tends to take from the Anglo-American world only that which helps to sustain the Pueblo people in a continuing, seemingly timeless existence.

Pueblo homes were originally without doors, with access by ladder from the upper floors. Corner fireplaces and dome-shaped ovens were derived from the Spanish. Floors were paved with stone slabs or plastered like the walls and roofs. The building material used in the western Pueblos is mostly stone held together with adobe mortar, the whole covered with adobe plaster. In the east, since the Spanish conquest, unmolded adobe brick has been used. The roof beams are usually cottonwood, pine, or spruce, with cross poles covered with brush and earth. By the twentieth century, modern tools and materials made possible larger rooms with the use of longer timber beams. The Pueblos were excellent basket makers; and their earthenware vessels, ancient and modern, include elaborately painted jars, bowls, and platters, each Pueblo often developing its own style.

The Pueblos, in common with many Indian peoples, think of Nature and God as one; they have traditionally revered the sky, earth, sun, and the subterranean "Great Ones," recognizing a group of supernatural spirits usually thought of as living under the world or in the sky and at the four cardinal points, or directions. These forces of nature, both cosmic—sun, moon, earth, wind, and fire—and animal spirits such as water serpents and spiders, or the dead, all

Above and Below: **Hopi, c. 1900. Traditional "butterfly" or "squash blossom" hairstyle symbolizing virginity; the hair is wrapped around two curved sticks into large whorls. Women who were married wore their hair tied with a cloth hanging down at the side of the head and over the shoulders. This post-puberty style is still occasionally seen.**

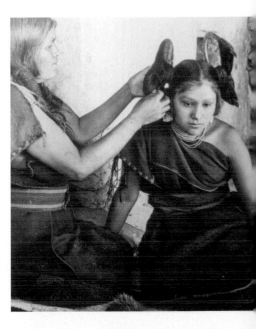

exhibit animal-like characteristics. These are friendly or hostile, requiring respect and worship by secret societies and fraternities, such as kachina or kiva societies, who dress in impersonation of the supernaturals during ritual dances to bring rain or good health. Such rituals usually take place in specially constructed semi-subterranean chambers known as kivas or on village plazas. These ceremonies are arranged in cycles according to the time of year.

The Kachina cult of the Hopi impersonates supernaturals, mostly cosmic forms, while animal impersonations are more common among the Rio Grande Pueblos—a reflection of their traditional reliance on hunting as well as farming. Ceremonies to please the animal spirits share the stage with saints' days where Catholicism has been more influential. Other societies included the Clowns (Koshares), who were sacred, as well as fun-making. Membership in these esoteric societies was granted by initiation at adolescence.

The Spanish introduced the official position of "Governor" at each pueblo as part of their colonial

Below: **Santa Clara Pueblo Buffalo Dance, 1990. The men wear buffalo headdresses and kilts decorated with the serpent symbol. The unmarried girls wear sun-disk bustles.**

administration, a political appointment sometimes passed on by descent, which continues today.

In 1885, the Indians of the nineteen Pueblos of New Mexico, including Zuñi, were reported as numbering 7,762, a drop from about 10,000 after the Pueblo Revolt of 1680. By 1946, this number had risen to about 14,500. By 2000, the people who ethnically identified themselves solely with one of the eighteen Rio Grande Pueblos in New Mexico numbered 33,918. An additional 1,840 Tewa-speaking Tigua people were affiliated with the Ysleta del Sur Pueblo in Texas. The Zuñi population stood at 9,094, plus 1,028 part Zuñi people. The Hopi people numbered 11,111, plus another 4,164 people who considered themselves part Hopi.

It should be noted that today, only a relatively small number of tribal members actually live in the historic Pueblo buildings. Many more live in the surrounding areas in modern housing.

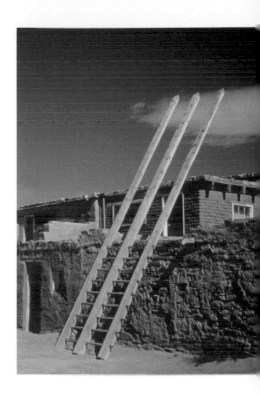

Above: **Acoma Pueblo, New Mexico, built on a high mesa, is now largely uninhabited except for festivals.**

ACOMA PUEBLO

The westernmost Keresan Pueblo and one of the most impressive, situated on a mesa almost 400 feet (122 m) high, some 50 miles (80 km) west of Albuquerque, New Mexico—sometimes known as "Sky City." A number of satellite communities have been established over the years at Acomita, Santa Maria de Acoma, and McCartys. Traditionally, the people share a basic culture with other Pueblo groups, particularly the Keresans, in social structure, religious and political systems.

The Acoma Pueblo vies with Hopi for the title of the oldest continuously inhabited village in the United States. Acoma pottery has hard, thin walls with white to yellow-brown glaze and is decorated with geometric motifs and parrot-like birds in overall designs. In 1956, the tribe numbered 1,888, rising to 2,512 in 1966. The third largest of the Rio Grande Pueblos, Acoma had a population of 3,956 in 2000.

COCHITI PUEBLO

A Pueblo village in Sandoval County on the west bank of the Rio Grande and the northernmost of

Above: **The northernmost Pueblo village in New Mexico, Taos Pueblo is six stories high in places. It was the closest Pueblo village to the Plains and was an important trading center.**

the Keresan-speaking villages. This small Pueblo witnessed all of the Spanish expeditions into New Mexico and took an active part in the Pueblo Revolt of 1680. A large number of people no longer live on the reserve, although they return for the feast of San Buenaventura in July, when the Corn Dance is performed. They are noted for creamy-yellow pottery with black designs and also for making cottonwood drums. They numbered 465 in 1956 and 799 in 1968. The 2000 population was 889.

ISLETA PUEBLO

A pueblo situated on the west bank of the Rio Grande 13 miles (21 km) south of Albuquerque, with an outlying settlement, Chiskal. The second of the three Southern Tiwa dialects of the Tanoan family is spoken by the inhabitants of this pueblo.

The Spanish destruction of Isleta religious chambers, masks, and other ritual items led to the Pueblo Revolt of 1680, which drove out the Spanish settlers for several years. Tribe members work in the surrounding communities, and at the Isleta golf resort and gaming facility. In 1956, they numbered 1,759, and in 1974, 2,710. In 2000, there were 3,652 tribal members.

JEMEZ PUEBLO

A Pueblo located on the Jemez River 30 miles (48 km) northwest of Bernalillo, in an area where several villages were reported by the sixteenth-century Spanish explorers. They were participants in the Pueblo Revolt of 1680 and suffered the traumas and punitive expeditions that followed. The people of this Pueblo speak Towa, a dialect of Tanoan. Although Native arts have weakened over the years, their political and religious organizations still function under a cacique (chief or leader) and his staff, who appoint the officers of societies, the moieties and clans. Like most Pueblo cultures of today, theirs is a mixture of Native, Spanish, and Anglo influences. The Jemez population stood at 1,137 in 1956, 1,939 in 1970, and 2,583 in 2000.

Above: **The Hopi Snake Dance, as depicted on a postcard of c. 1900. Photography has been banned at the ceremony for many years.**

LAGUNA PUEBLO

One of two western Keresan-speaking Pueblos and the largest of all Rio Grande Pueblos. Laguna had a population of 6,244 in 2000, up from 3,475 in 1956 and 5,800 in 1975. Tribal members occupy six villages at Paguate, Mesita, Encinal, Paraje, Seama, and Casa Blanca, plus the Laguna Pueblo 40 miles (64 km) west of Albuquerque. The Pueblo was founded in 1699. Their nearness to Spanish and Anglo towns in the nineteenth century resulted in some acculturation, but religious and secular officers (such as that of "governor," imposed by the Spanish in 1620) still follow the Keresan pattern despite internal groups with competing interests.

Below: **Two women from Isleta Pueblo. Farming has remained important to the Isleta until recent times, and they have produced a commercial style of pottery.**

NAMBE PUEBLO

A small Pueblo that has largely adopted Hispanic customs, 15 miles (24 km) north of Santa Fe, New Mexico, formerly speaking a Northern Tewa dialect of the Tanoan family. Women from this village once produced a good grade of micaceous (containing mica) cooking ware and wove belts of cotton. The present village is probably post-contact, but there are ruins of an earlier Pueblo close by. The population was 184 in 1956, 356 in 1972, and 441 in 2000.

Above: **Tesuque Pueblo Eagle Dancer, c. 1930. The Rio Grande Pueblos perform several animal dances involving impersonation and mimicry. The Eagle Dance— dramatizing the relationship between humans and the sky powers—has become a popular exhibition, performed by groups even as far afield as the northern Plains. The dancer wears a headpiece, gourd beak, and wing feathers.**

PICURIS PUEBLO

A small Tiwa-speaking Pueblo town 20 miles (32 km) south of Taos, New Mexico, with a population of 158 in 1956, 172 in 1972, and 254 in 2000. Good micaceous pottery has been traditionally made at Picuris. The Pueblo has been in the same vicinity as the present buildings since at least 1591. The Picuris are closely related to the Taos.

POJOAQUE PUEBLO

The smallest of the Pueblos, with incorporated Hispanic customs, and located 16 miles (26 km) north of Santa Fe, New Mexico. Their former language was a Northern Tewa dialect of the Tanoan family. Although archaeological investigations on the Pojoaque Reservation suggest a large population with extensive farming in ancient times, by 1712 they numbered only 79. In 1970, there were 46 residents and the 2000 census counted 211.

SAN FELIPE PUEBLO

The central village of the five eastern Keresan Pueblos on the west bank of the Rio Grande 10 miles (16 km) north of Bernalillo. They hold a special relationship to Cochiti and were perhaps once a single people, but there were villages in this area when Coronado passed through in 1540. Although few arts and crafts are now pursued, the secret societies function and ceremonials are still held. In 1956, they numbered 941 and in 1970 1,811. In Census 2000, the population was 2,606.

SAN ILDEFONSO PUEBLO

A Pueblo situated on the Rio Grande 20 miles (32 km) northeast of Santa Fe. They speak a Northern Tewa language of the Tanoan family, and claim descent from people who moved out of the valleys and cliff homes on the Pajarito Plateau. This Pueblo was involved in the Pueblo Revolt of 1680, and was one of the last to accept Catholicism in the nineteenth century. Since then they have often had internal conflicts between competing groups.

Maria and Julian Martinez, both famous potters, came from this Pueblo, producing a dull black paint on polished black ware. The Buffalo, Deer, and the Plains-oriented Comanche Dances are still performed at San Ildefonso's annual festival. San Ildefonso inhabitants numbered 138 in 1900, 413 in 1973, and 494 in 2000.

SAN JUAN PUEBLO

The largest and northernmost of the six Tewa-speaking Tanoan Pueblos, located 5 miles (8 km) north of Española on the east bank of the Rio Grande. It was in this vicinity that the Spanish founded their first provincial capital in New Mexico before moving to Santa Fe in 1610. The San Juan people suffered considerable persecution by the Spanish civil and church authorities until they rose in revolt in 1680. San Juan pottery is polished red and black ware with some incised and carved types. Their population was 934 in 1956, 1,721 in 1977, and dropped to 1,500 in 2000.

SANDIA PUEBLO

A pueblo 14 miles (23 km) north of Albuquerque. One of the three Southern Tiwa dialects of the Tanoan family is spoken by the people here. Although the site is a post-contact village, there are a number of prehistoric sites nearby. Sandia Pueblo was burned by the Spanish after the 1680 revolt.

Religion remains a means of keeping their identity in a location close to Anglo-Hispanic communities. They have retained the Corn, Eagle, Buffalo, and other dances, plus their *cacique* and governor. Mining, gaming, recreation and the arts fuel the economy. Their population was 74 in 1900, 265 in 1971, and 226 in 2000, making Sandia the second smallest pueblo.

Above: **A Pueblo Indian pottery maker, c. 1950. Maria Martinez from San Ildefonso Pueblo, New Mexico, was one of the most famous Pueblo potters of the twentieth century.**

Below: **A typical pueblo. Note the Spanish/Moorish-derived domed ovens in foreground. This artwork is modeled on Taos—compare it with the photograph on page 45.**

Above: **Acoma Pueblo, New Mexico.**

SANTA ANA PUEBLO
A small, conservative, Keresan-speaking Pueblo on the Jemez River 8 miles (13 km) from its junction with the Rio Grande, plus the village of Ranchitos. In 1956, they numbered 353, and in 1977 498. The 2000 population stood at 389.

SANTA CLARA PUEBLO
A Northern Tewa–speaking Pueblo town of the Tanoan family located on the west bank of the Rio Grande in Rio Arriba County, New Mexico. They traditionally lay claim to the cliff dwellings of Puye. The Pueblo occupies almost the same site as in the sixteenth-century. Santa Clara is often regarded as one of the wealthiest Pueblos, with a resource-rich land base that is a recreation attraction. The Santa Clara Indians make polished black and red pottery with modern variations. They numbered 669 in 1956, 1,204 in 1974, and 1,104 in 2000.

SANTO DOMINGO PUEBLO
A Pueblo located on the east bank of the Rio Grande 7 miles (11 km) south of Cochiti and the largest of the eastern Keresan Pueblos. Their ancestors probably occupied the Pajarito Plateau at one time. They have managed to maintain a core of basic Indian religion and beliefs; a cacique selects tribal, civil and religious officers for their dramatic ceremonials held in August. Pottery of varying quality has been made, as well as large amounts of jewelry. In 1956, they numbered 1,455, and 2,511 by 1970. By 2000, Santo Domingo was the largest Rio Grande Pueblo with 4,282 members.

TAOS PUEBLO
The northernmost Pueblo, located 10 miles (16 km) east of the Rio Grande and 70 miles (112 km) north of Santa Fe. Through most of the twentieth century, the neighboring town of the same name was a well-known artists' colony, and today Taos is one of the leading art markets in the United States. The Taos language is Northern Tiwa, a dialect of Tanoan. Traditionally one of the more prosperous

communities, surrounded by fertile farm land, this impressive multistory Pueblo is about six hundred years old. It is geographically close to the Plains Indians, from whom the tribe adopted elements of material culture—and recently the Peyote religion, which has caused much divisiveness. They numbered 1,137 in 1956, 1,463 in 1970, and 2,014 in 2000.

TESUQUE PUEBLO

The southernmost of the six still-functioning Rio Grande Tewa Pueblos, just 10 miles (16 km) north of Santa Fe, New Mexico. Despite their close proximity to Spanish and late Anglo-American influences, they have retained many ceremonials of ancient origin. They make their living from farming and pottery. In 1956, they numbered 185, 281 in 1973, and 383 in 2000.

ZIA (SIA) PUEBLO

A Keresan-speaking Pueblo on the Jemez River about 30 miles (48 km) north of Albuquerque. Presumably they are descendants of an older, larger Pueblo, "Old Zia." Although they have been nominally Catholic since 1692, a few traditional societies still remain. They have gained a livelihood in the recent past from grazing sheep and goats on surrounding lands. They are noted for making fine pottery with white or yellow-buff backgrounds and varied naturalistic designs of deer, birds, and leaves. In 1956, the Zia Pueblo had a population of 327, rising to 555 in 1972, 820 in 1992, and 1,590 in 2000.

ZUÑI

A tribe, a pueblo, and a linguistic family whose villages and present reservation are in McKinley County in the western part of New Mexico. Hawikah, one of their towns, was first seen by the Spanish in 1539; the following year Francisco Vásquez de Coronado captured the town during his expedition to find the "Seven Cities of Cíbola," perhaps the seven villages of the Zuñi. The Spanish were only partly successful in their attempts to convert and control the Zuñi, and in 1820 further attempts were abandoned, partly due to increasing

Above: **Acoma Pueblo, New Mexico.**

Below: **A Tewa guard at the top of the stairs to a kiva in San Ildefonso Pueblo, New Mexico.**

Above: **Santa Clara Pueblo men with blankets decorated with Plains Indian beadwork.**

raids on Spanish outposts by the Navajo and Apache. The heritage of Spanish contact was the adoption of some crops, horses, burros, and a system of secular government. Three summer farming villages—Ojo Caliente, Pescado, and Nutria—were established around Halona, the remaining central Zuñi Pueblo, and Tekapo, a fourth village, was established about 1912.

The Zuñis have been noted for their pottery, chalky-white slip with large brown-black designs, often depicting large rosettes, deer, frogs, and dragonflies, but the art has diminished in recent times. They also known for their turquoise and silver jewelry. Their social and religious organizations were composed of four interlocking systems of clans, the Kiva-Kachina society, the curing societies, and the priesthoods. The Shalako dance, a splendid portrayal of religious pageantry, is held in late November. The population has grown from about 1,500 at the beginning of the U.S. period in 1848 to 3,439 in 1956, 7,306 in 1970, and 9,094 in 2000.

HOPI PUEBLOS

Pueblos located on three mesas west of Kearns Canyon, the main administrative center for the Hopis. Hopi country is the southern escarpment of Black Mesa, a highland area about 60 miles (97 km) wide. Their present reservation, a square within the Navajo Reservation, is a continuing source of disagreement between the tribes concerning ownership. On First Mesa are the Tewa towns of Hano and Polacca, Sichomovi, and Walpi; on Second Mesa are Sipaulovi, Mishongnovi, and Shungopovi; and on Third Mesa are Bakabi, Hotevilla, Oraibi (along with Acoma Pueblo, possibly the oldest inhabited village in the United States), Upper and Lower Moenkopi, and Kykotsmovi. The Hopis speak a language of the Shoshonean family, now called Uto-Aztecan, and have lived in the same area of northeastern Arizona for over 1,600 years.

The basis of Hopi life in a harsh, dry environment has been the cultivation of corn, beans, squash, and melons, to which they added European fruits.

Spanish activity in the area was never extensive, although they contacted the Hopis beginning in 1540. They made various attempts to establish missions; but all churches were destroyed in 1680 and further efforts were dropped after 1780, leaving the Hopis in isolation to follow the indigenous culture lost to so many tribes. The tribe's experience with the United States began in 1848, when the Southwest territory was obtained from Mexico. This move initiated a series of factional splits, particularly at Oraibi, between conservative and liberal groups.

Hopi social structure contains a number of interlocking social and religious organizations, the latter exhibited in an annual cycle of masked Kachina rituals or unmasked ceremonials in kivas, or on plazas. The Hopis are renowned for their Snake Dance, held to bring rain for crops. Their pottery is characteristically a mottled yellow-orange with asymmetrical curved-line black designs. They are the only major basketmaking Pueblo tribe in recent times, mainly using flat coiled technique with abstract birds, whirlwinds, and kachina designs. In 2000, the Hopi population was 11,111.

Above: **Hopi dancers perform the Antelope Dance in this early twentieth century photograph.**

Below: **Taos Pueblo. Note the Spanish/Moorish-derived dome-shaped ovens in foreground.**

Below: **Mohave woman, c. 1880. Women originally wore only skirts of willow bark or, later, of cloth or yarn; some photographs show a large shawl, however. Hair was worn loose, and complex facial tattoos were common. Elaborate netted beaded collars were characteristic; a simpler necklace is worn here, with a Jew's harp hanging from it.**

A language family named after the Yuma tribe, located near the middle and lower Colorado River in Arizona, California, and adjacent Mexico. The Yumans traditionally had a relatively simple culture and were first exposed to Europeans in 1540 when the Spanish explorer Juan Ruiz Alarcón visited the area. Some Yuman groups were agricultural—the northwesternmost peoples to follow the Mesoamerican practice of maize (corn) farming.

Most River Yumans lived in low rectangular earth-covered houses, while the Maricopa adopted the round houses of the Pima. They grew corn, beans, and gourds, irrigated with floodwater runoff. The Upland groups ranged over a wide and arid territory, collected a variety of wild plant foods, and hunted. They lived in dome-shaped grass-covered shelters. Religion and ceremonialism were not elaborate; their beliefs were expressed through shamanism, curing by means of spirits, and dreams. The Yumans were often warlike and aggressive, but usually among themselves.

COCOPA (COCOPAH)
A tribe that lived at the delta of the Colorado River where it empties into the Gulf of California. They were typical River Yumans, but not always on friendly terms with the others. They numbered over 3,000 at one time, but fell to 1,200 in 1900. Two small reservations have been established near Somerton, Arizona. Farming remains vital to their economy, along with several other businesses, including gaming. In 2000, the total population was 808, with about half of that number living in Mexico.

DIEGUEÑO and KAMIA (Ipai-Tipai)
A people occupying San Diego County in southern California south of the San Luis Rey River. Originally called Kumeynay, they lived principally on wild plant foods, supplemented by hunting and fishing. They are grouped with the so-called Mission Indians, of both Yuman and Takic origin, who were associated with and under the control of the Spanish missions from 1769

until the missions were dissolved and their land dispersed during the 1820s and 1830s. By 2000, the number of people identified as Diegueño was 2,660, with another 1,057 claiming partial ancestry.

HAVASUPAI

An Upland Yuman tribe that occupied the plateau area on both sides of the Colorado River, including Cataract Canyon through which tributary Havasu River flows. Pressure for land during the nineteenth and twentieth centuries, and the creation of the Grand Canyon National Park, ultimately consolidated and restricted the Havasupai on a small reservation. Traditionally farmers, gatherers and hunters, they also excelled at basketry. Known to Spanish explorers in the sixteenth century, they changed little until the 1930s. In 1919, their reservation was reduced to 518 acres (209 ha), but restoration of original hunting land has since increased it to 189,113 acres (77,000 ha). By 2000, there were 576 Havasupais. Their economy is fueled by tourism and jobs in federal programs.

MARICOPA

A Yuman people of the River group, now concentrated along the Gila River. The Maricopa appear to be an amalgam of several older Yuman subgroups. Their present descendants are at Laveen on the Gila River Reservation and at Lehi on the Salt River Reservation, Arizona, both of which are primarily Pima reservations. The 2000 census reported 255 Maricopa and 150 with partial Maricopa ancestry.

MOHAVE (MOJAVE)

The northernmost Yuman tribe of the Colorado River group, living where Nevada, California, and Arizona adjoin. Although known to the Spanish from early on, they were too remote to be much affected by the missions. After the 1820s, however, they increasingly came into conflict with Americans. By the 2000 census, the Fort McDowell Mohave-Apache Community near Phoenix had 154 members, and the Fort Mojave Indian Tribe 1,906, including 1,437 who considered themselves solely Mojave. The Fort Mojave

Above: **A Mohave woman. The Mohave culture was traditionally of the simple desert Yuman type—plant gathering, some fishing, and hunting.**

LOCATION

The Yumans are located at the junction of three cultural areas: California, the Southwest, and Baja California. The Upland or Arizona Plateau branch is made up of the Havasupai, Yavapai, and Walapai, with the River branch consisting of the Mohave, Yuma (Quechan), Maricopa, Halchidhoma, and Kavelchadom. The Delta-California branch consists of the Diegueño, Kamia, and Cocopa; the Baja California branch, the Kiliwa.

Reservation is located along the banks of the Colorado River, in Arizona and Nevada. Agriculture—cotton, alfalfa, and wheat—is its economic base. There is a large casino at Fort McDowell, and the Fort Mojave people also operate two small casinos.

WALAPAI or HUALAPAI

A Yuman-speaking tribe of the Upland group, very closely related to the Havasupai and Yavapai and living in the Grand Canyon, particularly on the south side from the Coconino Plateau almost to the big bend of the Colorado River near Lake Mead. Contact with the Spanish began in 1776. Hostilities between the Walapai and Anglo-Americans in 1866 led to the destruction of their crops and their internment on the Colorado River Reservation. They later returned to their old lands and received a reservation of 1 million acres (405,000 ha). Originally gatherers and hunters, they now raise livestock. Their economy is fueled by tourism, timber, and art work. Their 2000 population was 1,419.

YAVAPAI

A Yuman tribe that occupied north central Arizona from the Pinal Mountains in the east as far north as Flagstaff, then west almost to the Colorado. Ultimately a reservation was established at Fort McDowell east of Phoenixs, with smaller reservations at Camp Verde, Middle Verde, Clarkdale, and Yavapai, near Prescott. The tribe has built gaming and other businesses. Although numbering over 1,500 before 1860, by 2000 there were only 818, plus 185 part Yavapai.

YUMA or QUECHAN

A people that lived at the junction of the Gila and Colorado Rivers in extreme southwest Arizona. They gathered wild foods and planted corn, pumpkins, and beans. In 1884, the government established the Fort Yuma Indian Reservation, although much land was lost during the allotments. Their original population was perhaps 4,000, but by 1937 it was only 848. The 2000 census lists 2,080 people who were solely Quechan and 532 with partial Quechan ancestry.

Below: **Yurok Jumping Dancer, c. 1896. Headdresses were made of redheaded woodpecker feathers and worn with buckskin aprons and dentalium shell currency necklaces; the latter were also carried in the elkhorn purse.**

An important, relatively large, and linguistically distinct tribe of northern California, living principally along the lower parts of the Klamath River between its junction with the Trinity River and the coast at Requa. They were part of a culture linking them to the Hupa, Karok, Tolowa, and Wiyot. Shamans, sometimes women, obtained power directly from spirits. World Renewal ceremonials were important, including the White Deerskin Dance, held semi-annually, alternately with the Jumping Dance. This was often performed by visiting Hupas, at Weitchpec in northwest California, where Northwest Coast cultural traits were influential.

Houses included the redwood plank type and ceremonial plank sweat houses. Facial tattooing, deerskin clothes, basketry, shell money, slaves, and wealth display traits paralleled the Hupa culture and, more remotely, that of the northern tribes.

Above: **A Yurok woman.**

The Yurok probably numbered in excess of 3,000 in pre-contact times, but were disrupted after 1827 when the first Hudson's Bay traders invaded their country, and clashes with gold-seeking whites occurred after 1850. However, the Yuroks retained some portions of their old land.

There have been recent attempts to revitalize their language and dances. Their salmon fishing tradition is dependent on California's management of water resources. They numbered 4,098 in 2000, with 1,711 people identified as part Yurok.

Above: **A Cahuilla man from Palm Springs, identified only as Marcos. The Cahuilla lived in rectangular and dome-shaped brush-covered shelters in small villages. Food consisted of small game, acorns, piñon nuts, beans, seeds, and wild fruits, with marginal agriculture providing corn and squash. They had a rich ceremonial life.**

ACHOMAWI or ACHUMAWI and ATSUGEWI

Together popularly known as Pit River Indians, as they occupied the Pit River basin from Big Bend to Goose Lake in north central California. Along with the Atsugewi, the Achumawi formed a branch of the Hokan family of languages. They fished for salmon, bass, catfish, and trout, caught wildfowl, and collected vegetable foods and insects. They suffered somewhat less than most Native Californians from white contact, and still numbered about 750 in 1963—perhaps half their original population. (The Atsugewi, however, were virtually annihilated by white settlers.) Many Pit River people still live in Shasta, Lassen, Modoc, and Siskiyou Counties. Census 2000 combined all of the Pit River people into a single group, with a total population of 1,656, plus 882 people of partly of the Pit River descent.

CAHUILLA

A large Takic-speaking (Uto-Aztecan) tribe closely related to the Cupeño, Serrano, and Kitanemuk, who lived in the mountains, canyons, valleys, and deserts north of the Salton Sea between the Little San Bernardino and Santa Rosa Mountains of southern California. Their population may have reached 6,000, but it was only 1,000 by the 1880s. By 1970, they numbered over 1,600. Census 2000 reported 2,142 Cahuilla and 1,046 part Cahuilla people.

CHIMARIKO

A small tribe and linguistic family that lived along a stretch of the Trinity River from its junction with the South Fork to Big Bar, in northern California. An influx of white miners in the 1850s and 1870s appears to have harmed the tribe. In 1849, they may have numbered 250; but only 9 survivors were found in 1903. The census of 2000 located 23 Chimariko and 22 part Chimariko.

CHUMASH

A major group of linguistically related people, now included in the Hokan stock, of Santa Barbara County, California, along the coast from San Luis Obispo to Ventura. They numbered perhaps in excess of 15,000 before the Spanish missions were established in 1772. The Spanish, determined to make farmers of the Chumash, mistreated them and destroyed their culture in the process. After the missions were closed in 1834, the Chumash merged or intermarried with Mexicans or were decimated by disease. One small reservation at Santa Ynez was set aside in 1855. By 2000, there were 4,032 Chumash, including 107 affiliated with Mission San Luis Rey in San Diego County and 70 at Santa Ynez in Santa Barbara County.

CUPEÑO

A small Takic-speaking tribe of the Uto-Aztecan family, who lived east of Lake Henshaw and west of the Santa Rosa Mountains in southern California. Closely related to the Cahuilla and religiously influenced by the Luiseño, the Cupeño probably numbered 500 when they first encountered the Spanish. Subsequently, they came under the control of the missions and were reduced to near serfdom. In 2000, there were 417 Cupeño, including 243 at the Agua Caliente Rancheria, and 151 part Cupeño.

ESSELEN

A tribe and small linguistic family related to the Hokan. They lived on the upper central coast of California from the Carmel River to Lopez Point. First contacted by the Spanish in 1602, the tribe declined with the destruction of the mission at Carmel in 1770, when they were absorbed by other missions. The Esselen may have numbered about 500 in the eighteenth century, but they were almost extinct by 1820. The tribe is still federally recognized, and by Census 2000 numbered 117.

GABRIELENO

A group that occupied an area now covered by the city of Los Angeles and adjacent islands. The Gabrielinos spoke a Takic language of the Uto-Aztecan family. They shared many of their arts with the Chumash and had developed a religion with named gods, such as Chingichngish, the erection of temples, and the use of vision-producing narcotics, which spread to neighboring tribes. They were missionized at the San Gabriel and San Fernando (Fernandeño) missions; diminishing in numbers from

Above: **Another photograph taken in the late nineteenth century of a Cahuilla man in Palm Springs. The Spanish passed through Cahuilla country in 1774, and the tribe was subsequently integrated into the mission system.**

Above: **The Gabrielino are named after Mission San Gabriel, founded in 1771, although Spanish explorers had contacted these people as early as 1520.**

Below: **Obsidian blade, set in a buckskin handle, used in the Brush Dance, Karok, northwest California, c. 1880. The Karok's principal rites were annual World Renewal ceremonials, similar to those of the Yurok and Hupa. The World Renewal rites and Brush Dances still survive.**

5,000 to a few hundred, they largely adopted Hispanic cultural and social traits. In 2000, there were 1,168 Gabrielino and 607 part Gabrielino people.

KARUK (KAROK)

A distinct tribe occupying the middle fork of the Klamath River in northern California, starting just north of the Yurok village at Weitchpec and extending northward to the vicinity of Seiad near the Oregon border. Their population was over 2,700 in the early nineteenth century. Except for a few groups of traders, the Karok had little contact with Euro-Americans until 1850–57, when a swarm of prospectors poured into northern California. The Karok displayed a similar culture to that of the Yurok, subsisting on fishing, hunting, and gathering wild plant foods. Houses were made from split log planks, canoes from hollowed-out redwood. They dressed in deerskins, heavily decorated with nuts and shells for ceremonial use. In Census 2000, 3,164 Karok and 1,737 part Karok were reported.

KAWAIISU

A small Uto-Aztecan tribe of the Numic branch that once lived in the southern foothills of the Sierra Nevada around Havilah, California. They were strictly a hunting and gathering people, similar in culture to their neighbors the Tubatulabal and Southern Yokuts. Except for puberty rites for boys and girls, ceremonials were few, although they had developed shamanism. They were probably contacted by the Spanish in about 1780; and their culture collapsed after trappers and farmers invaded their territory in the 1850s. Their original population was about 500, but the 2000 census identified only 4 Kawaiisu, plus another 4 with partial ancestry.

KITANEMUK

A small tribe of the Takic division of the Uto-Aztecan family, closely related to the Serrano. They lived on Tejon and El Paso Creeks in the western valleys of the Tehachapi Mountains in Kern County, California. Their culture was similar to those of the Tubatulabal and Yokuts. They appear to have merged with other Indians at the San Fernando and San Gabriel missions, but a few survived separately until the twentieth century around Fort Tejon and on the Tule River Reservation. They are no longer a recognized tribe.

LUISEÑO

A Uto-Aztecan tribe of the Takic branch, closely related to the Gabrielino, Cupeño, and Cahuilla. They lived between San Juan Creek and the San Luis Rey River in coastal southern California, in small sedentary villages who gathered plant foods, fished, and hunted. Houses were conical structures covered with reeds, brush, or bark. Their first recorded contact with Europeans occurred in 1796 with the founding of Mission San Diego, when they numbered perhaps 4,000; they were later missionized at San Juan Capistrano (Juaneño) and San Luis Rey. In 1834, the missions were secularized; following revolts against Mexicans and Anglo-Americans, the Luiseño suffered displacement and merged into the so-called Mission Indians. By 2000, there were 4,317 Luiseño and 1,248 part Luiseño people. In addition, there were 90 Juaneño people and 22 part Juaneño.

SALINA or SALINAN

A group of tribes formerly occupying the central coast of California and the rugged mountainous interior, from the upper Salinas River near the Soledad Mission almost to San Luis Obispo. There seem to have been two dialects which formed the Salinan language family, now tentatively included in the Hokan stock. They probably numbered over 3,000 before 1771, when the Spanish began missions among them, but their population was no more than 700 by 1831. This decrease continued after the secularization of the missions in 1834; only three families were known by the early twentieth century near Jolon, descendants of people associated with the San Antonio Mission. Census 2000 identified 366 Salinan and 315 part Salinan people.

SERRANO

A group of Takic speakers who lived east of Los Angeles in the San Bernardino Mountains. A northern group, the Vanyume on the Mojave River, are sometimes given separate status. Family dwellings were usually circular

Above: **Karok, pre-1870.** In northwest California, family or village feuds usually resulted in little more than retaliatory activity and might be settled by payment, with the parties acting out a formalized war dance. Male dress included moccasins for long journeys; warriors might add wooden slat armor. The principal weapon was the yew bow with sinew backing and string; syringa wood arrows were carried in shell-decorated fur quivers.

Above: **A Hupa apron. Although classified as a northwest coastal Athabascan tribe, the Hupa were probably the largest and most important Athabascan group in California. They lived principally along the Trinity River above its junction with the Klamath.**

willow structures covered with tule thatching; in addition, they had large ceremonial houses where chiefs or religious leaders lived. They made fine coiled baskets. Contact with the Spanish first occurred in about 1771, and they were collected into missions in about 1820. In 2000, there were 263 Serrano and 166 part Serrano.

SHASTA

A tribe in northern California that was culturally partly Californian and partly Plateau. The Shasta formed a Hokan language branch related to the Achumawi and Atsugewi. The Shasta proper occupied the upper fork of the Klamath River, Shasta River, and Scott River as far south as Callahan, California, and as far north as Jacksonville, Oregon. There were three small southern groups as well. The Shasta hunted deer and rabbits, fished for salmon, and collected acorns and wild greens. Houses were of low-roofed plank construction with side entrances, gathered into villages of five or six dwellings and a sweat house. They also used and obtained in trade buckskin, obsidian, dentalium shells, abalone, nuts, and woodpecker scalps. The Gold Rush and Rogue River Indian Wars shattered Shasta life and culture in the mid-1800s, and their population dropped from about 3,000 to only 100 or so by 1900. A few were incorporated on the Grand Ronde and Siletz reservations in Oregon and the Round Valley Reservation in California. As of 2000, there were 436 Shastas and 515 people of partial Shasta descent.

TUBATULABAL

A name for three small tribes in the upper Kern River valley, California: Bankalachi, Palagewan, and Pahkanapil (Tubatulabal proper). Although none of these remain federally recognized tribes, they once formed a linguistically separate division of the Uto-Aztecan family. They were first visited by Franciscan missionary and explorer Father Francisco Garcés in 1776. Expansion by the United States after 1850 completely disrupted Native life; a massacre by whites in 1863, and epidemics of measles and influenza, saw their population collapse from about 750 in 1850 to about 50 by 1970, with only 6

Native speakers left. Their descendants now live on the Tule River Indian Reservation or in the Kern Valley.

WAPPO

A group related to the Yuki and part of the Yukian linguistic family. They lived in the valleys of the Napa and Russian Rivers in Napa and Sonoma Counties in California, with a detached branch, the Lile'ek, on the south shore of Clear Lake. Their subsistence came from plant foods, river life, and small game. They excelled in basket making like their northern neighbors the Pomo. They were within range of the Spanish settlements and missions, and a number adopted Hispanic customs or style before American settlers moved in. In 2000, there were 108 Wappo and 140 part Wappo.

WASHOE (WASHO)

A tribe that inhabited the large valleys of the Feather, Yuba, and American Rivers of northeastern California and the areas north and south of Lake Tahoe from Honey Lake south to Walker River, in Nevada and California. They may belong distantly to the Hokan stock. Culturally they were midway between the true Californian and Great Basin cultures. The many rivers and lakes supplied them with fish; they gathered camas roots, pine nuts, and acorns that were cooked into gruel, and also hunted deer and mountain sheep. Houses were either conical, with bark slabs leaning against a frame of poles, or temporary dome-shaped brush structures. They were very fine basket makers of both coiled and twined weaves, and several became nationally well known. They numbered about 1,500 in 1850, and 725 in 1970. In 2000, there were 1,186 Washoe and 788 with part Washoe ancestry.

WINTUN (WINTU)

A group that lived on the west side of the Sacramento River valley from the river to the crest of the Coast Range and from Shasta County south to San Pablo Bay. They consisted of three distinct dialectic divisions: the Northern or Wintu division, the Wintun proper or

Above: **A Serrano woman. Like their neighbors the Serrano were gatherers, hunters, and fishermen. While the valley floors were largely desert, the upper mountain slopes provided streams and a food supply of nuts, acorns, berries, and small game.**

Below: **Wintu pit house. The peoples of the upper Sacramento River area spent part of the year in substantial circular earth-covered family lodges, about twelve to a village; larger versions served as men's assembly buildings and "Big Head" dance houses. They had one or more center posts and a ring of posts that supported beams and rafters covered with brush, bark, and earth. Access was by ladder via the roof smoke-hole.**

Nomlaki, and the Patwin or Southern Wintun. They were typically Californian in culture; their bark houses were gathered in villages around semi-subterranean earth lodges for ceremonials of the Kuksu type, including the Bole-Maru followers who performed the "Big Head Dance"—male and female spirit impersonators who wore impressive feather headdresses. By 2000, there were 2,058 Wintun and 1,821 part Wintun.

WIYOT

A small tribe on the coast of northwest California between the Mad and Eel River estuaries. They are now thought to be related to the Yurok, with whom they shared much of their culture, but the Wiyot were much more oriented to a coastal environment. There was heavy emphasis on salmon fishing and the hunting of deer, elk, and sea mammals. Their ceremonialism was the same as that of the Yurok and Hupa. They suffered a series of atrocities at the hands of whites, which reduced their population from 1,000 in 1850 to 131 in 1968. The 2000 census reported 444 Wiyot and another 230 part Wiyot.

YANA

A small linguistic family on the northeastern tributaries of the Sacramento River between Shasta Lake and Tehama. There were three geographical Yana groups plus the Yahi, a southern branch. Their population was perhaps 1,500 before a series of massacres by whites (c. 1850–1870) reduced their numbers to a mere 100 or so by 1910. There were still 42 Yana and 58 part Yana in 2000, but they have been considered extinct since 1916.

YOKUTS

A wide group of forty or fifty minor tribelets that spoke varying dialects within the Penutian family. They were the main people of the San Joaquin Valley south to Buena Vista Lake, east to the Sierra Nevada foothills and north to the Stockton area. They are divided geographically and culturally into three groups: the Northern Valley, Southern Valley, and Foothills Yokuts. The Yokuts were not a political group, their relationship being linguistic. All three groups made excellent basketry. Shamans had much influence, but the Kuksu cult did not extend to the core of Yokuts territory. The Ghost Dance movement of the 1870s had some converts. The Spanish encountered the Yokuts in the late eighteenth century, but the Spanish influence was greatest among the northern villages. The Mexican period, 1822–1846, saw punitive expeditions into Yokuts country, and final cultural collapse followed U.S. settlement in the 1850s. The Yokuts survived in isolated pockets throughout their territory; but epidemics and absorption into white communities dropped their population from about 18,000 in 1770 to 533 in 1910. The census of 2000 identified 2,924 Yokuts people, plus 1,572 who are part Yokuts. Many of these now live on small reservations (rancherias).

YUKI

A group of small tribes in the upper Eel River valley in the Coast Range of northwest California and also along the coast between Rockport and Fort Bragg. The Yuki proper lived in the Round Valley area; the Huchnom on the south Eel River; and the Coast Yuki in the coastal area. These tribes, together with the detached southern branch, the Wappo and Lile'ek, form a language family with no known relatives. Culturally the Yuki had a simple hunting and gathering lifestyle, but an elaborate ceremonial life. Their existence as an independent people came to an end in 1856, when white farmers destroyed the ecology of their valley homes. Many starved, or were killed by settlers. The establishment of the Round Valley Reservation in 1858 probably saved the handful of survivors. Some estimates put the original number of these three groups at over 8,000. By 2000, there were still 311 Yuki people and 254 who were part Yuki.

Below: The most celebrated Yahi was Ishi—"the last Yahi." He was found living near Oroville, California, in 1911 and was later befriended by University of California anthropologists Alfred Kroeber and Thomas Waterman. They provided him housing at the University Anthropology Museum in San Francisco until his death in 1916. During those five years, he provided a wealth of information about California's pre-contact Native culture. In the 1990s, Steven Shackley, a research archaeologist at the Hearst Museum of Anthropology, theorized that Ishi was actually a Wintun. This mask was made at the time of Ishi's death.

Allotment. Legal process, c. 1880s–1930s, by which land on reservations not allocated to Indian families was made available to whites.

Acculturation. Cultural modification of an individual, group, or people by adapting or borrowing the cultural traits or social patterns of another group.

Anthropomorphic. Having the shape of, or having the characteristics of, humans; usually refers to an animal or god.

Appliqué. Decorative technique involving sewing down quills (usually porcupine) and seed beads onto hide or cloth using two threads, resulting in a flat mosaic surface.

Apron. Male apparel, front and back, which replaced the breechcloth for festive costume during the nineteenth and twentieth centuries.

Bandolier bag. A prestige bag with a shoulder strap, usually with heavy beadwork, worn by men and sometimes women at tribal dances. Common among the Ojibwe and other Woodland groups.

Birch bark. Strong, thick bark used for canoes and various wigwam coverings. Used as well for a wide variety of containers that were also adapted for the European souvenir trade by the addition of colored porcupine quills, such as those produced by the Mi'kmaq and by the Ojibwe and Odawa of the Great Lakes area. Bark was an important resource, especially in the East, North and Northwest.

Buckskin. Hide leather from animals of the deer family—deer (white-tailed deer in the East, mule deer in the West), moose, or elk (wapiti)—used for clothing. Less commonly used for dress were the hides of buffalo, bighorn sheep, Dall sheep, mountain goat, and caribou.

Bureau of Indian Affairs (BIA). Begun in 1824, transferred from the War Department to the Department of the Inerior in 1849. Now, around half of the BIA's employees are Native American, and the Bureau provides services through its agencies in many big cities as well as on rural reservations.

Cacique. The chief or leader of a Native American tribe in the Southwest and other areas dominated by Spanish culture.

Coiling. A method of making pottery in the American Southwest, in which walls of a vessel are built up by adding successive ropelike coils of clay.

Confederacy. A group of peoples or villages bound together politically or for defense (e.g., Iroquois, Creek).

Cradles. Any of three main devices used across the continent to transport or carry babies: the cradle board of the Woodland tribes (cloth or skin attached to a wooden board with a protecting angled bow), the baby-carrier of the Plains (a bag on a frame or triangular hood with a cloth base folded around the baby), and a flat elliptical board covered with skin or cloth, with a shallow bag or hide straps, of the Plateau.

Drum or Dream Dance. A variation of the Plains Grass Dance adopted by the Santee Sioux, Chippewa, and Menominee during the nineteenth century. Among these groups the movement had religious features that advocated friendship, even with whites.

Ethnographer. An anthropologist who studies and describes individual cultures.

Hairpipes. Tubular bone beads made by whites and traded to the Indians, often made up into vertical and horizontal rows called breastplates.

Kachinas. Supernatural beings impersonated by costumed Pueblo peoples in religious ceremonial. Dressed kachina dolls instruct children to recognize the different spirits.

Leggings. Male or female, covering ankle and leg to the knee or thigh (male), usually buckskin or cloth.

Medicine bundle. A group of objects, sometimes animal, bird, or mineral, etc., contained in a wrapping of buckskin or cloth, that gave access to considerable spiritual power when opened with the appropriate ritual. Mostly found among the eastern and Plains groups.

Moiety. A ceremonial division of a village, tribe, or nation.

Pan-Indian. Describes the modern mixed intertribal dances, costumes, powwows, and socializing leading to the reinforcement of ethnic and nationalist ties.

Parfleche. A rawhide envelope or box made to contain clothes or meat, often decorated with painted geometrical designs.

Peyote. A stimulant and hallucinogenic substance obtained from the peyote buttons of the mescal cactus.

Peyote Religion. The Native American Church, a part-Native and part-Christian religion originating in Mexico but developed among the Southern Plains tribes in Oklahoma, which has spread to many Native communities.

Powwow. Modern celebration, often intertribal and secular, held on most reservations throughout the year.

Prehistoric. In a Eurocentric view of American Indian archaeology, Indian life and its remains dated before A.D. 1492.

Rawhide. Usually hard, dehaired hide or skin used for parfleche cases, moccasin soles, shields, and drum-heads.

Reservation. Government-created lands to which Indian peoples were assigned, removed, or restricted during the nineteenth and twentieth centuries. In Canada they are called reserves.

Roach. A headdress of deer and porcupine hair, very popular for male war-dance costume, which originated among the eastern tribes and later spread among the Plains Indians along with the popular Omaha or Grass Dance, the forerunner of the modern War and Straight dances.

Secularization of Missions. The 1834 breakup of California's Spanish missions, whereby Indians who had been forced to accept Catholicism and to labor at the missions were freed from service. Land that had been taken from the Indians was not returned as promised, however, but was instead distributed to Spanish settlers and other landowners.

Sinew. The tendon fiber from animals, used by Indians and Inuit as thread for sewing purposes.

Sweat lodge. A low, temporary, oval-shaped structure covered with skins or blankets, in which one sits in steam produced by splashing water on heated stones as a method of ritual purification.

Termination. Withdrawal of U.S. government recognition of the protected status of, and services due to, an Indian reservation.

Tobacco or pipe bag. Bags, usually buckskin, beaded, or quilled with fringing, made by most Plains peoples for men to carry ceremonial tobacco and pipes.

Tribe. A group of bands linked together genetically, politically, geographically, by religion, or by a common origin myth; a common language is the main reason. "Tribe" is itself a word that arouses controversy, with many prefering "Nation" or "People." Some "tribal" groups are only so described as a convenient tool for ethnographers studying collectively fragmented groups or collections of small groups of peoples who themselves recognized no such association.

War dance. Popular name for the secular male dances that developed in Oklahoma and other places after the spread of the Grass Dances from the eastern Plains-Prairie tribes, among whom it was connected with war societies. Many tribes had complex war and victory celebrations.

Weir. A brush or wood fence, or a net, set in a river to catch fish.

Wickiup. A rounded hut used in the West and Southwest, made from a rough frame covered in brushwood, grass or reed mats.

MUSEUMS

The United States naturally has the largest number of museums, with vast holdings of Indian material and art objects. The Peabody Museum of Archaeology and Ethnology at Harvard University, in Cambridge, Massachusetts, has over 500,000 ethnographic objects pertaining to North America, including a large number of Northwest Coast pieces. Many collections of Indian artifacts in major U.S. institutions were assembled by ethnologists and archaeologists who were working for, or contracted to, various major museums, such as Frank Speck and Frances Densmore for the Smithsonian Institution, Washington, D.C., or George Dorsey for the Field Museum of Natural History, Chicago.

Since the sixteenth century, the material culture of the Native peoples of North America has been collected and dispersed around the world. These objects, where they survived, often found their way into European museums, some founded in the eighteenth century. Unfortunately, these objects usually have missing or incomplete documentation, and because such material was collected during the European (British, French, Spanish, Russian) and later American exploration, exploitation, and colonization of North America, these collections may or may not accurately represent Native cultures. Collectors in the early days were usually sailors (Captain Cook), soldiers (Sir John Caldwell), Hudson's Bay Company agents, missionaries, traders, or explorers.

During the twentieth century, a number of museums have developed around the collections of private individuals. The most important was that of George Heye, whose museum was founded in 1916 (opened 1922) and located in New York City. It was called the Museum of the American Indian, Heye Foundation. This collection has now been incorporated into the National Museum of the American Indian, a huge building sited on the Mall in Washington, D.C., scheduled to open in September 2004. Other notable privately owned collections subsequently purchased or presented to scholarly institutions are the Haffenreffer Museum Collection at Brown University, Rhode Island; much of Milford G. Chandler's collection, which is now at the Detroit Institute of Arts; Adolph Spohr's collection at the Buffalo Bill Historical Center, Cody, Wyoming; and the impressive Arthur Speyer collection at the National Museums of Canada, Ottawa.

Many U.S. and Canadian museums and institutions have been active in publishing popular and scholarly ethnographic reports, including the Glenbow-Alberta Institute, the Royal Ontario Museum, Toronto, and, pre-eminently, the Smithsonian Institution, Washington, D.C. Most of the major U.S. museums have organized significant exhibitions of Indian art, and their accompanying catalogs and publications, often with Native input, contain important and valuable information.

In the recent past, a number of Indian-owned and -run museums have come into prominence, such as the Seneca-Iroquois National Museum, Salamanca, New York; the Turtle Museum at Niagara Falls, Woodland Cultural Centre, Brantford, Ontario, Canada; and the Pequot Museum, initiated with funding from the Pequots' successful gaming operation in Connecticut. The Pequots have also sponsored a number of Indian art exhibitions. Many smaller tribal museums are now found on a number of reservations across the United States.

There has also been much comment, debate, and honest disagreement between academics (Indian and non-Indian alike), museum personnel, and historians about the role of museums and the validity of ownership of Indian cultural material in what have been, in the past, non-Native institutions. Certain Indian groups have, through the legal process, won back from museums a number of funerary and religious objects, where these have been shown to be of major importance to living tribes or nations. The Native American Graves and Repatriation Act of 1990, now a federal law, has guided institutions to return artifacts to Native petitioners; some, such as the Field Museum of Chicago, while not strictly bound by this law, have voluntarily returned some remains and continue to negotiate loans and exhanges with various Native American groups. A listing of U.S. museums with Native American resources may be found at http://www.hanksville.org/NAresources/indices/NAmuseums.html.

FURTHER READING

Birchfield, D. L.(General Ed.): *The Encyclopedia of North American Indians,* Marshall Cavendish, 1997.

Brody, H.: *Maps and Dreams,* Jill Norman and Hobhouse Ltd, 1981.

Bruchac, Joseph: *Journal of Jesse Smoke: A Cherokee Boy: Trail of Tears, 1838.* Scholastic, Inc., 2001.

Buller, Laura: *Native Americans: An Inside Look at the Tribes and Traditions,* DK Publishing, Inc., 2001.

Coe, R. T.: *Sacred Circles: Two Thousand Years of North American Indian Art,* Arts Council of GB, 1976.

Cooper, Michael J.: *Indian School: Teaching the White Man's Way,* Houghton Mifflin Company, 1999.

Davis, M. B. (Ed.): *Native America in the Twentieth Century,* Garland Publishing, Inc., 1999.

Dennis, Y. W., Hischfelder, A. B., and Hirschfelder, Y: *Children of Native America Today,* Charlesbridge Publishing, Inc., 2003.

Despard, Yvone: *Folk Art Projects - North America,* Evan-Moor Educational Publishers, 1999.

Downs, D.: *Art of the Florida Seminole and Miccosukee Indians,* University Press of Florida, 1995.

Duncan, K. C.: *Northern Athapaskan Art: A Beadwork Tradition,* Un. Washington Press, 1984.

Ewers, J. C.: *Blackfeet Crafts,* "Indian Handicraft" series; Educational Division, U.S. Bureau of Indian Affairs, Haskell Institute, 1944.

Fenton, W. N.: *The False Faces of the Iroquois,* Un. Oklahoma Press, 1987.

Fleming, P. R., and Luskey, J.: *The North American Indians in Early Photographs,* Dorset Press, 1988.

Frazier, P.: *The Mohicans of Stockbridge,* Un. Nebraska Press, Lincoln, 1992.

Gidmark, D.: *Birchbark Canoe, Living Among the Algonquin,* Firefly Books, 1997.

Hail, B. A., and Duncan, K. C.: *Out of the North: The Subarctic Collection of the Haffenreffer Museum of Anthropology,* Brown University, 1989.

Harrison, J. D.: *Métis: People Between Two Worlds,* The Glentsaw-Alberta Institute in association with Douglas and McIntyre, 1985.

Hodge, F. (Ed.): *Handbook of American Indians North of Mexico,* two vols., BAEB 30; Smithsonian Institution, 1907–10.

Howard, J. H.: *Reprints in Anthropology Vol. 20: The Dakota or Sioux Indians,* J and L Reprint Co., 1980.

————: *Shawnee: The Ceremonialism of a Native American Tribe and its Cultural Background,* Ohio University Press, 1981.

Huck, B.: *Explaining the Fur Trade Routes of North America,* Heartland Press, 2000.

Johnson, M. J.: *Tribes of the Iroquois Confederacy,* "Men at Arms" series No. 395; Osprey Publishing, Ltd, 2003.

King, J. C. H.: *Thunderbird and Lightning: Indian Life in Northeastern North America 1600–1900,* British Museum Publications Ltd., 1982.

Lake-Thom, Bobby: *Spirits of the Earth: A Guide to Native American Symbols, Stories and Ceremonies,* Plume, 1997.

Lyford, C. A.: *The Crafts of the Ojibwa,* "Indian Handicrafts" series, U.S. BIA 1943.

Page, Jack: *In the Hands of the Great Spirit: The 20,000 Year History of American Indians,* The Free Press, 2003.

Paredes, J. A. (Ed.): *Indians of the Southwestern U.S. in the late 20th Century,* Un. Alabama Press, 1992.

Press, Petra, and Sita, Lisa: *Indians of the Northwest: Traditions, History, Legends and Life,* Gareth Stevens, 2000.

Rinaldi, Anne, *My Heart Is on the Ground: The Diary of Nannie Little Rose, a Sioux Girl, Carlisle Indian School, Pennsylvania, 1880* (Dear American Series), Scholastic Inc., 1999.

Scriver, B.: *The Blackfeet: Artists of the Northern Plains,* The Lowell Press Inc., 1990.

Sita, Lisa: *Indians of the Northeast: Traditions, History, Legends and Life,* Gareth Stevens, 2000.

————: *Indians of the Great Plains: Traditions, History, Legends and Life,* Gareth Stevens, 2000.

————: *Indians of the Southwest: Traditions, History, Legends and Life,* Gareth Stevens, 2000.

Swanton, John R.: *Indian Tribes of the Lower Mississippi Valley and Adjacent Coast of the Gulf of Mexico;* BAEB 43; Smithsonian Institution, 1911.

Early History of the Creek Indians and Their Neighbors; BAEB 73; Smithsonian Institution, 1922.

————: *Indians of the Southeastern United States;* BAEB 137; Smithsonian Institution, 1946.

————: *The Indian Tribes of North America;* BAEB 145; Smithsonian Institution, 1952.

Waldman, Carl: *Atlas of The North American Indian,* Checkmark Books, 2000.

Wright, Muriel H.: *A Guide to the Indian Tribes of Oklahoma,* Un. Oklahoma Press, 1951.

This index cites references to all six volumes of the Native Tribes of North America set, using the following abbreviations for each of the books: GB = Great Basin and Plateau, NE = Northeast, NW = North and Northwest Coast, PP = Plains and Prairie, SE = Southeast, SW = California and the Southwest.

Lumbee: 25, 54 (NE); 33, 53, 56 (SE)

Lummi: 11, 43–44, 45, 47 (NW)

Lushootseed: 47 (NW)

Lutuamian (Lutuami): 53 (GB)

Mackenzie Inuit: 31 (NW)

Mahican: 12, 13, 14, 15, 24, 26, 50, 52 (NE)

Maidu: 35 (GB); 7, 11, 22–23 (SW)

Makah: 11, 38–39 (NW)

Malecite: 11, 25, 27, 48, 54 (NE)

Maliseet: see Malecite

Manahoac: 11, 51 (SE)

Mandan: 8, 9, 11, 30, 32, 36–37, 40, 49, 50 (PP)

Maricopa: 11, 26, 27, 46, 47 (SW)

Mascouten: 11 (NE)

Massachuset: (Massachusett) 11, 51 (NE)

Mattaponi 57 (NE)

Matinecock: 12, 53 (NE)

Mattole: 11, 13 (NW)

Mdewakanton Sioux: 11, 45 (PP)

Meherrin: 23 (NE); 56 (SE)

Menominee (Menomini): 23, 53 (NE)

Mescalero Apache: 11, 13, 15, 16, 17–18 (SW)

Mesquakie: see Fox

Methow: 11, 53 (GB)

Métis: 27 (PP); 19 (NW)

Me-wuk: see Miwok

Miami: 11, 49, 51, 52 (NE)

Micmac: 52, (NW); 11, 25, 27, 28–29, 38, 48 (NE)

Mikasuki: 44, 45 (SE)

Miluk: 53 (NW)

Minitaree: see Hidatsa

Missisquoi: 50 (NE)

Missouri: 9, 11, 41, 51, 52, 53 (PP)

Miwok: 7, 11, 24–25 (SW)

Mobile: 11, 51–52 (SE)

Moctobi: 47 (SE)

Modoc: 11, 35, 52, 53, 54 (GB)

Mohave: 11, 46, 47–48 (SW)

Mohawk: 11, 19, 23, 24, 25, 30–31, 38, 56 (NE)

Mohegan: 11, 26, 48, 50, 52, 54, 56 (NE)

Mohican: see Mahican

Mojave: see Mohave

Molala: 11, 50, 54 (GB)

Monacan: 11, 52 (SE)

Monache: see Western Mono

Moneton: 11, 52 (SE)

Mono: 11, 24–25, 33, 35 (GB)

Montagnais-Naskapi: 26, 54–55 (NW); 48 (NE)

Montauk: 11, 48, 50, 53 (NE)

Muckleshoot: 11, 43, 44, 47 (NW)

Mugulasha: 47 (SE)

Multnomah: 11, 23 (NW)

Munsee: 12,14, 26, 35 (NE)

Muskogean: 7, 12, 24, 26, 28, 34, 39, 40, 42, 46, 48, 50, 51, 53, 54, 55, 56, 57 (SE)

Muskogee (Creek): 8, 35, 36, 49 (NE); 8, 10, 12, 17, 18, 28, 29, 32, 34–39, 41, 42, 43, 45, 46, 47, 49, 50, 57 (SE)

Na-Dene: 28, 48 (NW)

Nahyssan: 11, 52 (SE)

Nambe Pueblo: 39 (SW)

Nanaimo and Snonowas: 44 (NW)

Naniaba: 52 (SE)

Nansemond: 56 (SE)

Nanticoke: 11, 13, 15, 48, 50, 53, 57 (NE)

Napochi: 11, 46 (SE)

Narraganset: 11, 48, 50, 53, 56, 57 (NE)

Natchez: see Taensa

Natchitoches: 11, 46, 51, 52 (SE)

Nauset: 57 (NE)

Navajo: 12 (NW); 32, 45 (GB); 9, 11, 12, 17, 30–32, 34, 44 (SW); 32 (NE)

Nespelem: see Sanpoil

Nestucca: 47 (NW)

Netsilik Inuit: 31 (NW)

Netsilingmiut: 31 (NW)

Neutral: 11, 24 (NE)

Nez Perce: 21 (NW); 8, 10, 11, 26–30, 38, 51, 54, 57 (GB); 32 (PP); 15 (NE)

Niantic: 11, 53, 54 (NE)

Nicola: 11, 12, 18–19 (NW); 56 (GB)

Nipmuc (Nipmuck): 48, 54, 55, 56 (NE)

Nisenan: 22, 23 (SW)

Niska: 50 (NW)

Nisqually: 11, 44, 45, 47 (NW)

Nooksack: 11, 44, 47 (NW)

Nootka: see Nuu-chah-nulth

Norridgewock: 50 (NE)

North Carolina Algonkians: 54 (NE)

Northern Athabascan: 15–20, 41 (NW)

Northern Ojibwa: 25, 26, 40–41, 54 (NW); 37, 40, 48 (NE)

Northern Paiute: 24, 25, 31, 33, 34, 35, 50 (GB)

Northern Shoshone: 36, 37, 38, 39, 50 (GB)

Nottoway: 11, 23 (NE)

Ntlakyapmuk: see Thompson

Nugumiut: 29 (NW)

Nutka: see Nuu-chah-nulth

Nuu-chah-nulth: 5, 6, 10, 38–39 (NW)

Nuxalk: 11, 21, 36, 42, 45, 46 (NW)

Occaneechi: 11, 51, 52–53 (SE)

Oconee: 50 (SE)

Ofo: 11, 47, 53, 54, 55 (SE)

Ojibwa: 40–41 (NW); 8, 9, 10, 27, 28, 29, 40, 55 (PP); 8–11, 20, 32–37, 40, 41, 48, 54 (NE)

Okanagan: 53, 54, 55 (GB)

Okchai: 34 (SE)

Omaha: 8, 11, 39, 40, 45, 52, 53, 55 (PP)

Oneida: 11, 13, 19, 22, 23, 24, 26, 34, 38, 50 (NE)

Onondaga: 11, 19, 23, 24, 30, 38–39 (NE)

Opelousa: 47 (SE)

Oregon Penutian: 53 (NW)

Osage: 8, 11, 39, 40, 51, 52, 53 (PP)

Oto (Otoe): 8, 11, 40, 51, 52, 53, 54, 55 (PP)

Ottawa: 8, 11, 14, 17, 32, 36, 40, 41, 48, 49, 54 (NE)

Owens Valley Paiute: see Eastern Mono

Ozette: 11, 39 (NW)

Padlimiut: 29 (NW)

Padouca: 12 (SW)

Paiute: 11, 24, 25, 31–35, 37, 39, 40, 42, 43, 50. 52, 56 (GB); 6 (SW)

Pakana: 34 (SE)

Palouse: 11, 48, 53, 54 (GB)

Pamunkey: 57 (NE)

Panamint: 24, 25, 39, 41 (GB)

Papago: see Pima

Parklands People: 28 (PP)

Pascagoula: 11, 53 (SE)

Passamaquoddy: 11, 25, 27, 48, 50, 54, 55 (NE)

Patwin: 8, 56 (SW)

Paugusset: 55 (NE)

Pawnee: 8, 9, 10, 11, 12, 22, 38–39, 48, 50, 52 (PP); 15, 44 (NE)

Pawokti: 12 (SE)

Pawtucket (Pawtuxet): see Pennacook

Pecos Pueblo: 11, 34 (SW)

Pedee: 11, 53 (SE)

Pennacook (Pawtucket): 50, 51, 55 (NE)

Penobscot: 27, 50, 51 (NE)

Pensacola: 11, 53 (SE)

Pentlatch: see Puntlatch

Penutian: 26 (GB); 7, 22, 24, 56 (SW)

Peoria: 51, 52 (NE)

Pequawket: see Pigwacket

Pequot: 11, 43, 48, 50, 52, 55, 56 (NE)

Petun: 11, 16, 23 (NE)

Piankashaw: 52 (NE)

Picuris Pueblo: 40 (SW)

ABOUT THE CONTRIBUTORS

Richard Hook (Illustrator and Contributing Author
An internationally respected professional illustrator specializing in historical and anthropological subjects for more than thirty years, Hook has had a lifelong interest in Native American culture that has inspired his remarkable artwork. He has been widely published in the United States, Europe, and Japan. A lifelong interest in Native American culture led to his selection as illustrator for the Denali Press Award-winning *The Encyclopedia of Native American Tribes*.

Michael G. Johnson (Author)
Johnson has researched the material culture, demography, and linguistic relationships of Native American peoples for more than thirty years, through academic institutions in North America and Europe and during numerous field studies conducted with the cooperation and hospitality of many Native American communities. He has published a number of books, in particular the Denali Press Award-winning *Encyclopedia of Native American Tribes*.

Bill Yenne (Contributing Author)
Involved in publishing for over 25 years, Yenne lives in San Francisco and is the author of over 100 books, many on American Indian subjects.